LEARN TO LIVE

LEARN TO LIVE

A New Thought Interpretation
of the Parables

By ERVIN SEALE

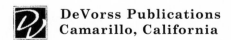

DeVorss Publications
Camarillo, California

Learn to Live
Copyright © 1955
by Ervin Seale

ISBN: 978-087516-652-0
Fourth Paperback Printing, 2009

DeVorss & Company, Publisher
PO Box 1389
Camarillo CA 93011-1389
www.devorss.com
Printed in the United States of America

To all my friends and students everywhere
whose "ears have heard" and whose "eyes have seen"

PREFACE

THIS BOOK IS THE OUTCOME of my classes and lectures on the Parables over a period of years. There have been many books on the Parables, but comparatively few for the layman, one of the most extensive studies of the last generation being *The Parables of Jesus* by George A. Buttrick, Harper and Brothers, 1928. Among the more recent writings on the subject has been *New Man* by Dr. Maurice Nicoll of England. This last is a brief introduction to the language, the technique and significance of the Parables along with some of the miracles of Jesus. However, as Dr. Buttrick, quoting Arnot, points out: "(Each) century must produce its own literature, as it raises its own corn, fabricates its own garments . . . the intellectual and spiritual treasures of the past should indeed be reverently preserved and used; but they should be used as seed . . . We should cast them into the ground and get the product fresh every season—old yet ever new."

It is exactly in this spirit, and from this point of view that I offer my book on the Parables of Jesus.

By hybridizing we have found that there is much more in a kernel of corn than our grandfathers knew or were able to bring forth. The potentialities were always there. We have created nothing. We have merely brought another potentiality to light and to usefulness. The new and vital science of psychology, even though it crosses swords with religion on many points, nevertheless has done great service to religion, having rediscovered certain truths about man and his mental-emotional process—truths which in part at least were known to other generations and cultures in the form of myths, allegories and religious dogma. In spite of the fact that a psychology based on a materialistic way of life must perforce create confusion and wallow in it, modern psychology and its offshoots have made many original and valuable contributions. Many of the old truths have thus been re-clarified and made practical for the present time, just when we are most in need of them. This is good for the twentieth-century mind. Ours is an age in which religion and science have moved ever closer to marriage. Scientists of the physical world have at last found themselves at the end of matter and in the realm of invisible particles of light. Many readers have concluded, after reading the works of scientists like Jeans and Eddington, Compton, Milliken and Einstein, that these men are mystics, having a perception of two worlds at once. The practical discoveries of these men and their colleagues in the atomic age have given a dramatic and fearful urgency to the need for morality and human knowledge to come together as a higher wisdom. Doctrines and beliefs and theologies are not sufficient today, if they ever were sufficient. Today it is right action that counts, and that right speedily. A growing proportion of men and women are no longer interested in what you believe about Christ or God or religion, or salvation after death, but what can you do now to make life easier and happier and more significant, and therefore more worthwhile for all time and eternity. Can you act out the beliefs of your religion? This has always been a problem throughout the ages. Man's belief has always been better than his act. Our ideal always has trouble becoming real, but those sacred writings which set forth the ideals of the human race also show how to realize them. In other words, there is science or practical working knowledge in them. The Parables, significantly, not only illustrate what human conduct should be, they reveal in their subtle way how to do the thing that we see should be done.

In the conviction that this realization is the pressing need of our time and in the awareness that the Parables are timeless, and that no expositor can do better than to apply them to his time, this book on the Parables of Jesus is offered here.

The Bible quotations are all from the King James Version.

ERVIN SEALE

CONTENTS

PREFACE 7

WHAT IS A PARABLE? 15

YOUR MIND—The Kingdom of Heaven

1 THE SERMON BY THE SEA OR THE KINGDOM OF HEAVEN
PARABLES 27
    The Parable of the Sower
    The Parable of the Wheat and the Tares
    The Parable of the Mustard Seed
    The Parable of the Seed Growing Secretly
    The Parable of the Leaven
    The Parable of the Hidden Treasure
    The Parable of the Pearl of Great Price
    The Parable of the Dragnet

THE LAWS OF THE MIND

2 HOW THE MIND WORKS 107
    The Parable of the Labourers in the Vineyard
    The Parable of the Talents
    The Parable of the Ten Virgins
    The Parable of the Wedding Robe
3 RENEWING THE MIND 135
    The Parable of New Cloth and the Wineskins
    The Parable of the Wicked Husbandman
    The Parable of the Rejected Cornerstone
    The Parable of the Wise and Foolish Builders

The Parable of the Unfinished Tower and the
King's Rash Warfare
The Parable of the Rich Young Fool

SETTING THE LAW IN ACTION

4　THE LAW OF USE　　　　　　　　　　　　159
The Parable of the Two Sons
The Parable of the Barren Fig Tree
The Parable of the Children at Play
The Parable of the Candle

5　IMPORTUNITY OF THE LAW　　　　　　　181
The Parable of the Importunate Widow
The Parable of the Importunate Friend
The Parable of the Rich Man and the Beggar

6　SKILL AND FORESIGHT IN APPLYING THE LAW　194
The Parable of the Unrighteous Steward
The Parable of the Unmerciful Servant
The Parable of the Two Debtors
The Parable of the Good Samaritan

THE LAW IS A PERSON

7　OBEDIENCE AND HUMILITY　　　　　　　221
The Parable of the Chief Seats
The Parable of the Pharisee and the Publican
The Parable of the Unprofitable Servants
The Parable of the Travelling Householder
The Parable of the Lord's Return from the
Wedding

REALIZATION AND ATTAINMENT

8　THE LAW OF LIFE　　　　　　　　　　　243
The Parable of the Lost Sheep and the Lost Coin
The Parable of the Prodigal Son

LEARN TO LIVE

WHAT IS A PARABLE?

A CERTAIN MAN'S BUSINESS was dying. He could see nothing but ruin ahead. One day, in his despair, he got into his car and drove out into the country, aimlessly. It was the spring of the year and freshets were running. The river had overflown its banks and had left little pools of water in the meadows in which schools of glittering fish were stranded, unaware of the fate in store for them. The pools of fish caught the man's eye and he stopped his car to examine them more closely. It was sad to think that these bright little fish would die as soon as the pools of water dried up. The man got down on his hands and knees and began digging little ditches whereby the fish could swim back to the main stream. While he was absorbed in this benevolent work for the fish, the thought suddenly occurred to him, "Why, I am God to these fish. Without me they would surely perish. I am their saviour, I am their God." And then came a second great realization to this man. "There must be," he thought, "a greater power and wisdom which is God to me and which will save me from perishing. Of course there is. I will go back." Renewed confidence surged through him, and he did go back, and in time recouped his fortunes.

I have just related to you a modern parable. Let us analyze it for a minute. First of all, it indicates very plainly and very dramatically that a change of the individual mind is the only difference between misery and happiness, success and failure. Whenever a constructive influence enters into a person's mind, that person will see a way out of his trouble and will thenceforth make progress speedily. This book is to help you to find certain truths which will so influence your mind that you, too, can renew your confidence and find the way to a good life. A parable is a story especially designed and written to accomplish this change in your mind, and, consequently, in you.

In the story just related about the business man, there are two dominant ideas. The first one is the man's kindness toward the fish. The second one is the idea of the providence of a greater wisdom and power working toward man's welfare. The first idea induced the other. A parable is a form of writing that tells a story about common everyday things within the range of every individual's experience, and at the same time draws a subtle analogy between the ordinary facts of the story and the deeper meaning which lies parallel to the facts. Literally, the word parable means, "a comparison." It is from the Latin, *parabola*, which in turn is from the Greek word which means "placing beside, to compare; similitude." Every parable is, therefore, two stories placed side by side, or two meanings thrown beside each other for comparison. There is a similitude between them, and the Bible reader will recall the frequent expression in the teachings of Jesus: "The Kingdom of Heaven is like unto" or "To what shall I liken it" and "It is like."

Thus, in every real parable, you have two stories: one is literal; the other is figurative. They lie right alongside each other, and one suggests the other. One is evident and obvious; the other is induced by thinking upon the first.

All outer facts are parables implying inner facts. Misery and happiness are not of this material world alone, but have their counterparts which are generated in the mind. We speak of coincidence, that is, two like things happening at the same time but in different places, as though it were a rare occurrence and the exceptional thing. But two things are always happening together in this life. Thought and act are always side by side, as are mood and experience. Life is a parable, for it has its two sides always parallel.

The Parables of Jesus are the greatest parables in all our literature. They speak of vineyards, stewards, coins, fish, flour, seeds and sowers—all the basic elements and aspects of life in His time. They are as charming, direct and applicable today as they were nearly two thousand years ago.

All sacred writing has a science to it. The science of the parable is in the technique of creating a two-fold story. If only one of the stories is obvious to the literal-minded reader, to him, therefore, there is no great wisdom or instruction in a parable. Solomon compared such a mind to a lame man: "As the legs of a lame man are not equal, so is a parable in the mouth of a fool."

The parable is a psychological mechanism, a mental transformer. It is designed to do things to the mind of the reader or listener, to help him coordinate psychological and physical truth. Our actual circumstances and our idealized version—what we would like them to be—do not agree. Desire and fact quarrel in each one of us at times, and we spend the days in inner conflict. In fact, all despair and discouragement are simply states of mind which are brought about when we give more power to circumstances than we do to our own ability to change and modify circumstances. When the literal facts get the upper hand and plunge the ideal into temporary submission, then despair and frustrations result. At such a time, if the ideal or the positive wish of a person can be aroused and raised up, it will take command of the situation and subdue the domineering facts, modify them and change them. All therapy for the human mind must somehow lay hold of this principle and encourage, by whatever means, the positive wish for life and better life in the individual. A man must learn to look at this life and see the relationship between what he is doing and what he is thinking; otherwise he is lame, and a lame man makes progress slowly.

If the parables fall upon our ears but do not awaken their higher meaning in us, they do not teach and cannot help us. We see only one side of the story. We hear the parables as apt little tales which illustrate the right or wrong conduct of life, but nothing more.

Let me illustrate: a messenger travels between the offices of a thirty-story building every day. He does so by means of the elevator and his feet. The elevator is a moving floor. All the other floors are fixed and stationary. If the messenger is on the tenth floor and he wants an office on the twentieth floor, he cannot cause the twentieth floor to come down to where he is, but he must take his own floor with him to the twentieth and equalize them there, make them one, that is. It is so with our minds and with life. We cannot bring the higher meaning down to our present level of consciousness. We must take our own consciousness up to the level of those meanings and understand them where they are, for what they are, in the way in which they are. It is always a change in ourselves that matters, and the parable is designed to work this inner change. If you read it and meditate upon that part which you readily understand, it will cause your mind in time to perceive its higher parallel.

It frequently takes an extremity in a person's life to open up his hearing to the higher truths. The man who helped the fish was in great extremity, and that is why he saw the parallel between what he was doing with his hands, and what life is always trying to do with everyone of us, that is, help us. But if the man had not come to misfortune in suffering, but rather had gone along serenely, satisfied with what he was and what he was doing, the chances are his mind would never have awakened to see the parallel between the spiritual meaning and the physical act.

This does not mean that we always have to suffer in order to grow, but it does mean that we have to be dissatisfied with our old selves before we can accept any portion of our newer and higher selves. Suffering is the imposition of life's will to growth and progress upon man's stubborn and self-satisfied ego. If a man can understand himself and can voluntarily let go of old things and welcome the new, he will not have to suffer. But if he stubbornly clings to his opinions and beliefs, to his methods and habits, then at some point life will force a change. We all suffer in this life. There is no escaping it. But the amount of suffering that anyone of us has to endure, depends upon how hard of hearing we are. Life is eloquent with assurances of health and happiness. But human ears have been long accustomed to hearing the counsel of fear, and hearing talk of trouble and sickness. The mind is tuned to the wave length of difficulty and suffering, and the vibrations of the good life fall futilely upon ears that are too dull to hear.

That is why, as we shall see, the first parable is about hearing. It is as simple as the Scripture says, the ears and the eyes and the heart must be opened to the reception of a higher truth, and then healing takes place.

Therefore speak I to them in parables: Because they seeing see not; and hearing they hear not, neither do they understand.

And in them is fulfilled the prophecy of Isaiah, which saith, By hearing ye shall hear, and shall not understand; and seeing ye shall see, and shall not perceive:

For this people's heart is waxed gross, and their ears are

dull of hearing, and their eyes they have closed; lest at any time they should see with their eyes, and hear with their ears, and should understand with their heart, and should be converted, and I should heal them.

Matthew 13: 13-15

All outer change must follow inner change. The only obstacle standing between a man and a new order of things in his mind, his body and his affairs, is his dullness of hearing, his inability to hear some new and finer interpretation of things as they are. This inner change is called hearing, and if we listen well and correctly to the parables, we will be able to affect the necessary changes in our outer life.

He speaks to them in parables, the Bible says, but they seeing see not and hearing hear not. What does this contradictory statement mean? It is obviously an observation of the fact that every parable has a double meaning. The ordinary mind hears the ordinary meaning of the parable, its story content, but cannot hear or perceive its secondary meaning. Such a mind hears but hears not, and sees but sees not. The outer and ordinary meaning of the parable is obvious and common to the average mind, like the story of a man going on a journey and telling his employees to take good care while he is away. This part of the parable makes good sense, for we have just such situations today, and we recognize the rightness of a hired man doing his job while the boss is away. And, per contra, we deplore the idea of an employee who is dishonest, faithless and slovenly. He shirks his duties especially when the boss is not looking. Such an account bears some relationship to everyday life as we see it today. It appeals to our reason and to our good sense. It is an object lesson showing the difference between right and wrong in the employer-employee relationship. This much is easy to hear. But after nearly two thousand years of this parable's teaching, not every employee today is faithful, or diligent, or industrious. Not every employee is honest when his boss is away. In fact, we might guess that the degree of honesty at this level of half-hearing does not change much from year to year and from generation to generation, because such a level of mind has no ability to change until it hears the message of its higher self. Talk to the average person at this level of awareness and he will agree with you that honesty is the best policy. But he will not always practice it, because he can't. He is in that state of mind which perceives itself in a world of many forces and powers, a world of chance, fate, and malevolent entities; according to its perception it concludes that it must thrust and parry and jocky for position, get while the getting is good, kill or be killed. A person enacts the role of his own nature inevitably. He expresses what he is. He can do no other. You may have a beautiful philosophy, you may have lofty ideals, but what you will do with your philosophy and ideals is dependent entirely upon what you are inside yourself. What you are compels what you do. This is the tragedy of most of the world all through the ages; that it cannot do what it sees should be done. Because it has not seen nor heard the higher meanings of life, and therefore has not awakened the higher powers within itself, it has no ability or capacity to do the higher things.

We can all have whatever appeals to us as desirable, but the way to get it is not by picking it up wherever we may see it because it may belong to somebody else, and he may not want to dispense with it just yet. There is another and a better way of getting what we want. That infinite intelligence deep inside you which gave you the desire will also give you the capacity and the wherewithal for getting what it bids you to get. But this calls for understanding on your part. You will have to rise higher than the mere childish perception of things and relationships into an understanding of yourself and your psychological and spiritual capacities and powers. "Surely nobody," says Emerson, "would be a charlatan who could afford to be sincere." But you cannot afford to be sincere unless you know your higher self and its strength and capacity. So the mind which fails in positions of trust or honor is the mind that sees but does not see, and hears but does not hear. Nevertheless, says Jesus, "I speak to them in parables," because the parable, when understood on both its levels, will open your mind to the perception of the higher meaning, and you will see and hear and realize your potentialities.

> . . . without a parable spake he not unto them . . .
>
> Mark 4:34

All that is required of an individual to be converted and healed, that is, changed round so that he faces in a positive direction, is that he have his eyes and his ears open so that his heart, or his feelings, are no longer stonelike and fixed in definite patterns, but flexible and melted down and ready to flow into new channels.

A parable is not the same thing as an allegory, though they are often confused in some people's understanding. A parable deals with real things on two levels. An allegory, on the other hand, deals with real things on one level. The Garden of Eden story, for example, is an allegory. No one, as Origen, the Church Father, points out, has ever seen a tree of life and a tree of the knowledge of good and evil growing in an orchard or on a lawn. There are no such actual trees. These are therefore fictitious trees, from an objective point of view. But this is a way of describing ideas which start as seeds in the mind and then grow up into strong, fixed and established patterns, bearing fruits in attitudes and actions. And hence the expressions, tree of life, and tree of good and evil, are figures which stand for very real and important things in our psychology and in our living. Bunyan's *Pilgrim's Progress* is a perfect example of the allegory. There was no such actual man as Christian, or actual people called Evangelist, Faithful, Hopeful and Giant Despair. These are types of character and human conduct. They represent or stand for qualities, characteristics and patterns of action in all of us. As actual individual people they are fictitious, but as capacities within the human nature and characteristics, they are everlastingly real.

A fable is another form of narrative which may sometimes be confused with the parable, but a fable is different from a parable in this respect. The fable deals with irrational animals and inanimate objects as though they were personalities. The myths speak of flying horses and beings who are half-horse and half-man. Fables tell of wolves that talk, and trees and flowers which can act. The myth teaches divine truths. The fable teaches common sense and virtue. But in each case the myth and the fable uses unreal things to speak of real things. The exceptional and outstanding difference between the parable and all other forms of speaking and writing is this: it is dual in its meaning, and both meanings are real and rational. A father who had two sons, one wise and one stupid, is a real and actual situation which we observe every day. But that every person's mind is the father of two distinct kinds of attitudes, two different ways of thinking and feeling and acting, is not always so quickly and clearly observed. The two meanings are parallel and it is this parallelism which constitutes a parable. Upon understanding one side and meditating upon it, our mind opens to perceive the other. The world's greatest teacher of things spiritual used the highest art of the teacher, the parable. For the parable does not fill the mind with descriptive facts, but opens the seeing eye and the hearing ear until the mind is aware of the treasures it already possesses.

While the parables are so universal and contain so many facets of understanding of the law, it is not possible to force them into strict categories or groupings. Some of the parables belong in several classifications because they apply equally well to more than one heading. Yet each parable has a dominant theme and the dominant themes as I see them are here set down as chapter headings which reveal the progressive development of that science of understanding as Jesus taught it.

YOUR MIND

THE KINGDOM
OF HEAVEN

1

THE SERMON BY THE SEA

OR

The Kingdom of Heaven Parables

THE PARABLE OF THE SOWER

And he spake many things unto them in parables, saying,
Behold, a sower went forth to sow;

And when he sowed, some seeds fell by the way
side, and the fowls came and devoured them up:

Some fell upon stony places, where they had not
much earth: and forthwith they sprung up, because
they had no deepness of earth:

And when the sun was up, they were scorched; and
because they had no root, they withered away.

And some fell among thorns; and the thorns
sprung up, and choked them:

But other fell into good ground, and brought forth

fruit, some an hundredfold, some sixtyfold, some thirtyfold.

Who hath ears to hear, let him hear.

.   .   .   .   .   .

Hear ye therefore the parable of the sower.

When any one heareth the word of the kingdom, and understandeth it not, then cometh the wicked one and catcheth away that which was sown in his heart. This is he which received seed by the way side.

But he that received the seed into stony places, the same is he that heareth the word, and anon with joy receiveth it;

Yet hath he not root in himself, but dureth for a while: for when tribulation or persecution ariseth because of the word, by and by he is offended.

He also that received seed among the thorns is he that heareth the word; and the care of this world, and the deceitfulness of riches, choke the word, and he becometh unfruitful.

But he that received seed into the good ground is he that heareth the word, and understandeth it; which also beareth fruit, and bringeth forth, some an hundredfold, some sixty, some thirty.

Matthew 13:3-9, 18-23

Parallel passages: Mark 4:2-8, 13-20, and Luke 8: 4-8, 11-15.

THE SERMON ON THE MOUNT in Matthew 5, 6 is known to millions. The Sermon by the Sea in Matthew 13 is less well known. The Sermon on the Mount contains the condensed teaching of Jesus in epigrammatic form. The Sermon by the Sea is entirely in parable. Of the nine parables found in the Sermon by the Sea, eight are found in the single chapter of Matthew, 13. Actually, all the parables in the gospels are kingdom of heaven parables, but we classify fourteen of them especially as kingdom of heaven parables because the term is actually mentioned or used somewhere in the text. Eight of these comprise the Sermon by the Sea.

The kingdom of heaven is the burden of Jesus' teaching and he used parables to show what the kingdom of heaven was like. Before taking up the parables, let us try to grasp the concept of the kingdom of heaven, for on it hangs all the meaning of the teaching of Jesus. Jesus in his teaching lets it be known that he is in this world but not of it. He is a citizen of another realm. His power, his authority and his nourishment come from that other realm that is not distant in time and in space from the realm in which other humans live, but is rather simultaneous and coexistent with the life of all of us. Only a relatively few attain the kingdom and those few can enter in and live in that realm only after preparation and education.

Now, a kingdom is a form of government, and if the reader will remember that in the days when the gospels were written the kingdom was almost the universal form of government, it will help him to understand this term as it is used in the Bible teaching. Today we know what a republic is, or a representative democracy, or a dictatorship, or a totalitarian form of government, and in some countries we have seen what is called an oligarchy in which a certain group out of the population makes the laws and runs the country. We know what a limited monarchy is—one in which the monarch rules and reigns largely in name only. But in the old-time kingdom the king's wish was law, his will was absolute. The king was the only power. There was no opposition. So a kingdom as it is used in the Scriptures means a rule or an authority with total, supreme and unlimited power.

But this is the kingdom of heaven that we are talking

about, and heaven means the spiritual or immaterial world. If matter means form and shape, then the formless and shapeless is not matter, but is immaterial, or spiritual. And this can only be mind or consciousness, with its function of thought and feeling. Heaven is the opposite of earth, and earth is the realm of embodiment. It is in this realm of mind that Jesus, without scepter, robe or crown, without visible throne, palace or retinue, holds his sovereignty. It is in the realm of mind and consciousness that the Christ man is king of kings and lord of lords. And it is into this realm as a king, ruling with authority and grace, that the Christ teaching seeks to bring every man. While it is a paradox from an earthly point of view to make every man a king, from a spiritual or heavenly point of view it is no paradox at all. For every man is inherently a king and must one day take note of his heritage, put himself under the proper tutelage, and once more assume the throne of his own life.

A good man with wisdom ruling in his mind holds all evil at bay. He "blunts the edge of the sword, and turns alien armies to flight." Failure, sickness, hatreds, resentment, and bitterness, and all human problems will yield to the authority and sovereignty of wisdom ruling in the human mind. Wisdom, then, is the real king. And when it sits enthroned in a human consciousness, that human consciousness is king on earth, as wisdom is king in the heaven of his mind. That you may take control of your own thought, marshal its forces, and destroy its enemies, and live in harmony with all of your surroundings, is the Bible teaching. And the Parables of Jesus are illustrations to help you accomplish this task.

Since the kingdom of heaven is nonphysical it is beyond description, therefore no one can point out definite paths of travel, or give precise rules and formulae. The spiritual world is invisible, therefore we cannot see it with the eyes, therefore we cannot describe it with the mind. In telling another man about this realm of kingship within himself where he may take control of his own mind and therefore his own world, we have to work through parables saying it is like this, or it is like that, or it resembles this other thing, in order to force the mind to think within itself and to discover something within itself, and to curb the mind in its ever hungry tendency to look outward, to mistake a symbol for the truth.

If we were instructing a person how to become a monarch in the external, physical world, we could give him precise instructions. If you wanted to be an actual monarch, for example, we should have to tell you that you should have arranged a long time ago to have been born into one of the few remaining royal families. Hence you would have been placed under tutelage and instruction which would have fitted you to rule and to reign. But since that is out of the question for most of us, there are other ways in which we can become kings and queens. You can become a king in oil or cotton or wheat, or a queen among poets and novelists. A specialist in any field is a kind of monarch in that field. And there are schools and forms of instruction available to give you knowledge and skill in these fields. But in the kingdom of heaven the school is yourself, your own mind and its processes. Since we are all as individualistic as the whorls on our fingertips, we cannot set up one rule or formula by which all people can reach the kingdom of heaven. That is why all fixed formula and frozen creed becomes like the stones in a graveyard, monuments to death, immobility and inaction. Life is fluid, always moving and always going somewhere. But there is a technique which all people can use to make progress toward the assumption of their role of authority in the kingdom of heaven, and that technique is the parable. It is a psychological tool designed to help the mind to open its inner sight, and to see its own capacities and treasures.

The Parable of the Sower

Only those who have lived close to agriculture before the days of mechanization, or who have given some careful thought to it, will grasp the clear picture of the parable. A modern farm machine sows in precise, measured rows, and a modern farmer wastes no seed by the way side. But in the days before drills and seeders, a farmer had to sow his grain by hand. The method is called broadcasting. The farmer carries the bag of seeds slung over his shoulder, and with one hand he reaches into the bag and gets a handful of seed, and then with a gesture resembling that of a person throwing grain to the pigeons in a city park, he scatters the grain upon the prepared surface of the land. Naturally, in such an operation the farmer cannot control precisely the fall of the seed. As he walks near the edges of his field some of it is bound to fall by the way side and among the brambles and the thorns. On the other hand, within the center area of his field there are bound to be certain areas which are stonier than others, or wetter, and therefore not as capable of producing. And while the farmer may try to avoid planting in these areas, a few seeds are bound to fall upon these spots. In the Western world, where farming is now largely mechanized, this method of sowing grain is now the exception, and is practiced only by small farmers and gardeners. But in many lands across the face of the earth, this ancient and natural way of sowing seeds in the soil is practiced with every return of the sun.

This is the picture the parable presents to us, a familiar picture of a familiar operation. Now let us find the higher meaning of the parable; the nonliteral meaning.

God, or wisdom, is like the sower and he sows this world and all that is in it with the truths of life. They are being broadcast all the time, everywhere. They are continually falling upon our minds like grain upon a field. As the atmosphere of this world is full of radio programs produced by man, so the ether is full of the emanation of the Most High. The cosmic rays which descend upon our earth out of space are said to penetrate through eighty feet of lead, but the truths of God penetrate everywhere. What our minds individually do with the seed that falls upon them is determined by the nature of our minds. Our minds are like the soil. Different minds are of different composition, of different quality and state of development. This is represented in the parable by the different kinds of soil, and this point is so important that some have been led to rename this parable and call it the parable of the soil.

If the seed is the same, but the soils are different, you will get varying yields and quality of products in accordance with the quality of the soil. As I write this I am eating peaches from different trees of my own planting. The two trees were planted in two different soil types. The size and appearance, the history of growth, and the final product of the trees make an interesting comparison and an eloquent example of the fact that differing soils will bring from the same kind of seed a different product.

Putting it more precisely, certain soils allow the seed to express its potentialities more fully than others. The analogy to our lives is, then, that human beings make different and variable responses to the truths of life. Every human mind has its history, its conditioning, its training. These furnish the light by which that mind sees its world. Some people are actually color-blind and cannot distinguish red from purple. Others are tone-deaf, an unthinkable limitation to a musician, but not an item of major concern to the rest of us. Every court of law knows how unreliable witnesses can be. Three different witnesses reporting the same accident will relate different details. One says that the man driving the second car wore a brown hat. The other says the hat was black. While the third may remember no hat at all.

The truth of the situation is always there, impinging upon the minds of all onlookers, but what each mind does with that truth makes up the kaleidoscopic variety of human nature. All the senses of man are thus fallible. We neither see nor hear nor taste nor touch nor feel what is actually there. We see or hear or taste or touch or feel what is there plus what we are. As regards the sense of touch, the old story of the blind men who examined an elephant is typically true. One felt the ear and said the elephant was like a fan. Another felt the side and said the elephant was like a wall. Another felt his tail and said the elephant was like a rope. One felt the leg and said the elephant was like a tree. To a being with twenty-five or thirty senses beyond our own, the five-sense man must seem worse than blind. What we are is always getting in the way of what we feel and what we do. What we are qualifies and conditions what we see and what we hear, and the way we respond to different people and to different events.

The parable of the sower stresses the fact that different kinds of soil make different responses to the same seed in order to show us that different kinds of minds respond differently to the truth. But before we go that far we must also recognize that different kinds of minds make different responses to every situation, whether true or not, and when we see this we cannot be too surprised to discover that different minds see and hear the truth differently. Other people, events, situations, circumstances, sights and sounds of our environment set off our response mechanism and cause us to respond automatically. For example, two women are chatting, and one says, "My dear, when Alice said she didn't like my new spring suit I just went all to pieces." Now why should a remark by one person cause another person to go to pieces? Because there are psychological mechanisms in the second person all ready to be set off, or to say it another way, she is conditioned and primed and all ready to explode. A psychological mechanism is only an established pattern of thought and feeling. If you establish a pattern of inferiority in your thinking, you are bound to be set upon by critical remarks of others. If, for example, you do not trust your own good taste in dress, you are bound to hear a number of remarks such as those which Alice made about her friend's dress, and these remarks will set you going into a tizzy whenever you hear them. If, on the other hand, you have established a healthy pattern of trust in your own good judgment in matters of dress, and if you feel comfortable in the things you choose to wear, then another person's critical remarks will not awaken any emotional response in you at all, except perhaps pity for the one who is critical.

A classical example of this was given years ago by Coué when he was explaining this very point. "Suppose," said Coué, "you are on board ship and you walk up to a passenger who is making his first trip across the ocean. He has heard and read many tales of seasickness and is therefore not too sure how he, himself, will react. You say to him, 'You look a little pale, do you feel ill? Are you sure you are all right?' and so forth. Your words will trigger off his natural predilection for seasickness, and he is likely to have trouble soon. Go next to an old salt who has sailed the sea for many years and say something similar to him. What response will you get from the old sailor? Your words will serve only to call more forcibly to consciousness the man's immunity to seasickness, which is his own conviction based upon his own long experience. He will respond to your words in terms of his own strength, whereas the other responded to your words in terms of his own weakness.". Coué explained all this as the action of suggestion upon two different human minds. Suggestion is a term which is still bandied about among psychologists and metaphysicians with not too much understanding. If the reader will study these examples carefully he will discern that neither suggestion nor hypnosis can be correctly understood as the act of exercising control over another mind by communicating some idea, belief or picture to the other mind. There just is no such thing. All control is always and forever within the individual mind. There is never any departure from this.

When you are down on yourself, the world will maul you. When you are up on yourself, the world will bring you baskets of blessings and lay them at your feet. You cannot be chased unless you run. But you, and you alone, determine what the outside world will do with you. "All judgment is given unto the Son," as Jesus puts it, and the "Son" means the mind of man, for the mind is the offspring of the universal spirit. Therefore all judgment and determination about your personal life is given unto you. You, and you alone, determine what emotional responses you will make to the sights and sounds of your environment.

These two, judgment and response, form the balanced equation of all life. The prophet Zechariah (4:13-14) calls them the two anointed ones that stand by the Lord of the whole earth.° Let us take another example from everyday life. In this instance two men are talking, and we overhear one saying, "Did he burn me up!" And here again we notice that the remark or the action of another person has called forth a violent emotional response, and there is apparently no attempt on the part of the responding person to check the violence of his emotional response. An ugly

° See pp. 27-33 of my *Ten Words That Will Change Your Life.* Also p. 131.

thought has awakened a demon, and the person who has
been moved to an outburst or a slow, smoldering, burning
inside, is apparently powerless to do anything about it. At
first we are all like this. At first we are all like the old town
bell which used to hang in the town square. The rope hung
there beside it and anyone who came along might tug at it
and sound the bell. Of course, actually this didn't happen
often because citizens of the town knew that the bell must
not be sounded lightly or in jest. But in ourselves a good
many vagrants ring the bell. Our thought is like the rope
which awakens the sounds of the bell, and by misguided,
ignorant thinking we may sound off at times to our own disturbance and to the disturbance of our neighbors.

The thing to do, obviously, is to find some standard around
which to do your thinking until you build a life of your own
which is impervious to the attacks of the world around you.
This will put your bell rope out of the reach of vagrant hands
and will make it impossible for anyone else or any circum-
stance or situation to molest or to disturb the peace and poise
and harmony of your own nature. The parables can help to set
up this standard, and give us faith in the real power within.
For the mind of real faith does not look to circumstances for
encouragement. It does not blow hot or cold as the tide in
outward affairs changes. If the mind changes when circumstances change, then the mind has no stability and therefore
it has no faith. Faith, is alluded to in the Scriptures as a
rock. And a rock is stable. It is hard and impervious. It is
solid and relatively immovable. Truth alone is a rock upon
which and by which the mind should build its structure. Of
one thing we can always be sure and that is that the
external world is always changing. We cannot put our foot
upon anything and say this shall endure. So that if we depend for stability upon the outside world we shall surely be
lost. We shall be the hapless victims of change. But the

man of real faith, while working with the external world, is independent of it. He does not think that things or people or events can either harm or hurt him. He takes his cue for life and his confidence from another source. That source is his knowledge of the spiritual law, which the Bible calls wisdom, more precious than rubies, more to be desired than fine gold. It is translatable into every form of external good, but it is not any one of those forms in and of itself.

The person who has this wisdom in clear realization and in strong conviction stands relatively unmoved in the swirls and eddies of outward change. His mind draws confidence from what he knows, not from what he sees. Therefore his confidence is constantly being renewed and replenished, and he stands strong and assured in the midst of every discouraging situation. He knows that the tide which bore away some fortune at evening will return it tenfold in the morning. He holds all things loosely, for his treasure is not in things but in principles. Such a mind can endure.

The average man's reaction to politics, to religion, to persons, to business, to labor or to capital, is usually not determined by his personal conscious judgment of the hour, but by some subconscious emotional prejudgment of the past. His conditioning determines his reaction. He repeats the bromides, the clichés, the fears and the joys of the crowd. The emotional life of many of us is largely prejudice. The word prejudice means prejudgment. It indicates, therefore, a reaction of mind and emotion which has been set up or determined by a previous order of thought rather than by the thinking of the moment. Our parents and our teachers, our heredity and our environment, set up certain emotional patterns in all of us, and these determine how we react to situations of the moment. The outside world is full of ideas and events and opinions. These all affect us, to be sure, but they affect us suggestively. That is, they influence us by suggesting that we follow in their mode. But every individual has the capacity and the power to accept or to refuse suggestion. What response we make individually to popular prejudice or propaganda of the hour depends upon what kind of a person we are inside ourselves. If we are of that group which is never so happy as when it is discussing its ailments, we are much more likely to be affected by the weather, by germs and bacteria, and by talk about actuarial tables, than we otherwise would be. By such talking and thinking we have long conditioned ourselves to believe in outside influences and as a man thinketh in his heart so is he, or so he experiences. It is not only difficult, it is impossible, for any of us to know or to experience anything outside of our own consciousness. What we have thought most about, that we shall surely see everywhere in the world about us. What we have neglected to think about or to experience in our thought, we shall most certainly never see in the world outside of us. We may scoff at the news that others have seen it or are experiencing it. We may even scoff at the suggestion that it even exists. There are none so blind as those who will not see. And "seeing" is a state of mind. It is a condition of consciousness. The hypnotized subject, seeing a dog or an empty chair where none exists, is a dramatically extreme example of the normal state of each and every one of us.

We walk in a world of our own creation. The world we see is the world we are. Each of us lives in his own private world and sees things and activities just a little bit differently from the way his neighbor sees them. In a very real and scientific sense, each of us lays down the sidewalks and erects the buildings as he passes, and creates every tree and flower, full-grown, as he looks upon it. The phenomenal world is somewhat every individual person's creation. And that is one good reason why it is so difficult to get men to agree.

The building of the tower of Babel was not an isolated instance in history, but it is a perennial and therefore a present-day occurrence. Because I project my own world out of my own consciousness, and you similarly project yours, what is brick to me may be straw to you, and vice versa. It is the soil of my own mind which produces that green tree in the yard, and it is the soil of your own mind which produces that green tree for you. You and I take it for granted that we see the same tree, but we don't. The tree that I see is the tree that is actually there plus the amalgamation of all that my mind has read, heard and experienced of trees. And so it is with your mind. We are individual soil types giving rise to different kinds of growth within our consciousness and experience.

But, you may ask, is there no reality beyond our own individual, mental experience? Is the tree actually there and is the tree something in itself apart from what you and I see it to be? Yes, of course, there is a real tree, an actual tree, and it is this reality that first impinges upon our consciousness. What we do individually with this reality forms our particular awareness and experience.

The parable stresses this truth when it says that the seed falls indiscriminately from the hand of the sower upon all types of soil. The seed is reality, but reality is always qualified and conditioned by the mind that regards it. The tree is something in itself. But this reality impinges upon and is filtered through the individual consciousness and emerges as something less than reality. The botanist sees one kind of tree. The lumberman another. And the landscape gardener still another. Each person's mind responds to a different combination of qualities and characteristics in the tree, of reality. The archetypal world of truth and reality is all about us, falling like seed constantly. It is the infinite abundance of all things good and true and beautiful and just and right,

because it is the unity of all things. And it is unity simply
because it has not yet passed into the diversity, which is human experience. As the rain falls upon the just and the unjust, and the sun shines upon the good and the evil man
with equal generosity, so the seeds of truth fall upon the
variable minds of men. The different kinds of mind among
men are like the different kinds of soil in the parable.

The parable points out that there are basically four different types of minds, illustrated by the four different soil types
mentioned. First of all, there are the minds that are generally unresponsive. These are the minds of those whom Dr.
Sell calls the hard-surfaced people.* They are represented
in the parable by the wayside where some of the seed fell
and the fowls of the air quickly ate it up. That is, it had no
chance to take root. The wayside is the road over which
animals and men and vehicles pass. It is hard and impacted
from much travel. It is not porous or friable. It is unreceptive even to the rainwater which can penetrate only an inch
or two. Such minds are unresponsive for a number of reasons. In this class is the cynic, the skeptic and the dogmatist,
all of whom generally refuse to accept anything new. They
have long ago hard-surfaced their mind with certain opinions
and beliefs and refused even the rain from heaven. These
are the unteachables who have closed their minds and have
said there is nothing more to learn, I refuse to disturb my
comfortable opinions. These are the ones who prompted
Job to say: "No doubt ye are the people, and wisdom will
die with you."

In this class, too, are the negative minds, what Dickens
called the "dark, damp, dank souls," who meet every ray of
sunshine by sending up a dark cloud from themselves. Every
beam of light which approaches them must be filtered
through their fog bank first. Their negative dispositions, long

* *Studies of the Parables of our Lord* by Henry T. Sell, D.D. (Revell).

schooled in the philosophy of defeat and failure, shoot down every winged inspiration like Parsifal bringing down the swan. Some of these negative people are not willfully so. They have merely fallen into bad habits, bad training and bad environmental influences; have closed the doors and windows of their minds where they live in a small dark cubicle of limitation and lack of faith. Like recluses they barricade themselves against the outside world and do not even dare to believe that there is any light or joy beyond that which filters through the chinks and cracks of their house. The negative mind is schooled in negatives. It works overtime with the word no, but rarely says yes to anything. It shoots down the white birds of inspiration and sends forth the black birds to eat up the promises and the prophecies of good things to come. Present the negative mind with a positive idea and it will proceed to pick it apart and destroy it. It will not give the positive idea time to work upon the mind. Like the seed which falls upon the hard-surfaced ground, it disappears quickly.

The second kind of soil that is illustrated by the parable is the stony ground. "Some fell upon stony places where they had not much earth, and forthwith they sprung up because they had no deepness of earth. And when the sun was up they were scorched, and because they had no root they withered away." And this is so with certain types of enthusiastic, emotional people. These are the minds who respond readily enough to any good idea or positive program, but who cannot follow through. And the world has always reserved its honors for the people who follow through. The old fable of the tortoise and the hare is a well-known portrayal of how perseverance and following-through wins rewards. The hare type of mind is usually one of great capacity and natural endowment. It often has great versatility, with talents that call in many directions. It could succeed in any one of these directions, if it had the will to follow through, but it rarely does. Every person who has managed or worked with people recognizes the type. They are quick to grasp the significance of a proposition. They can discuss it brilliantly. But they cannot follow through. Finally, in despair, the director or the manager will have to turn to a slower, duller type of mind which has to be worked over and worked with very strenuously in order to get it to see a course or program of procedure. But once it sees it, tortoise-like, it plods remorselessly forward and achieves the goal.

The extreme idealists follow right along in this category, also. By extreme idealists I mean those who deal too exclusively with their ideals and not enough with the embodiment of those ideals. We should all be idealists striving constantly to transform our ideals into the reality of everyday. But the extreme idealist says, "I go," as in the parable of the two sons, but he does not go. He gets lost in the contemplation of going. He may become so lost, so entranced in his own meditation that he forgets where it was he was to have gone. Then, too, the pure idealist cannot reconcile the ideal world which he sees as a possibility with the real world which seems always to stand in the way of the realization of that possibility. The real world wears him down. The everyday rough and tumble of affairs discourages him and causes him to lose heart. He does not believe enough in the spiritual principle of the capacity, the innate capacity, of the ideal to make itself real in spite of all seeming material opposition. His roots do not go down deep enough into reality. He does not understand the spiritual principle of mental causation: as we think, so we are. He believes that physical things cause other physical things. In short, he believes in matter and materialism. He thinks that what he sees obstructs what he feels. And so, in dealing with the

external world of hard, real fact, he—to use words of Jesus
when he interprets the parable of the sower in the gospel—
"dureth for a while." No wise man ever said that it was an
easy thing to maintain faith and confidence and joy in the
face of discouraging circumstances, but if the mind has nothing more to sustain its faith and to maintain its confidence
than the signs and the evidence and even the miracles of
external life, then indeed it has no root and it dureth for a
while.

The pure idealist who has not reconciled his ideals with
the world of events and forms and processes, who cannot see
that absolute and relative are one world, who tries vainly to
deny the real world in order to set up a world of his own, is
in continual conflict within and without. His insights or
roots do not go deeply enough into the fundamental soil of
the principle of life, so he cannot endure the battle. His
ideals are continually rising like a fountain from within, but
circumstances are continually frustrating them from without.
His mind draws his substance from two directions and when
they clash, the resultant emotional storm, like raging water,
bears his hopes away.

But before the parable mentions that good soil, which
implies the good mind, it has one more type of poor soil to
consider. Some seed, the parable says, fell among thorns, and
the thorns sprang up and choked them. This illustrates the
mind that does not keep up its daily mental treatment or prayer
work in order to keep itself in healthy, constructive and positive condition. For as the seed of God is broadcast upon the
earth, so the seed of the evil one is also broadcast upon the
earth. This does not mean that there is an actual devil going
around sowing negative thoughts in people's minds; it
merely means that for every affirmative idea there is an opposite or negative one. Every yea has its nay. If you think
of yourself as possessing a certain blessing you can also

think of yourself as void of that blessing. If you are not well grounded in the spiritual law and do not have confidence in your ability to choose, then these two opposites will quarrel in your mind and in most cases fear will get the better of faith and choke out the good seed. If this is your present experience you must diligently school yourself to pray daily until you invoke the power which will help you to sustain constructive thought and imagery. You cannot think two opposite thoughts at the same time. The attempt to do so will cause them to cancel each other, and vitiate all constructive, concerted movement. This is the law in metaphysics, just as in physics the law is that two things cannot occupy the same place at the same time.

Agriculture is a continuous battle against extraneous growth. A good farmer has always been known by the cleanness of his field. It requires hard work, but it produces results. And it is results which we want in all cases. Good scientific prayer is no less hard work in its way than getting up at dawn and dragging a harrow across a field until sunset. If you would keep your mind clean of the negative thoughts which debilitate and weaken, you must be constantly at it.

Dr. Buttrick has pointed out that "there is a gradual ascent in quality of the three types of character" illustrated by the three types of soil. "The first is impenetrable, the second shallow, but the third is rich earth with possibilities of a generous harvest." Here is rich and fertile soil containing all the elements necessary for good production, but it has thorns in it. The growing thorns will rob the grain of nourishment. A farmer with such a type of field did not harrow and disk enough before he planted his crop. He did not rid his field of the extraneous growth. The mind that is illustrated by this condition of soil is called the preoccupied one, and such it is. A preoccupied mind has a previous occupant, which gives no wholehearted welcome to a new arrival. It sits in the background and shadows of the mind, feeding upon substance of the mind and withholding it from the proper occupant. For example, a man wishes to fill his mind with positive convictions of progress and happiness, but he is holding on to an old grudge or resentment. An old resentment or a sleeping inferiority puts a drag upon his best efforts. The energy of his mind is divided between two opposites.

When Jesus interprets this parable he says that the thorns represent the cares of this world and the deceitfulness of riches. What are the cares of this world? They are the concerns of the mind with the happenings and movements and sensations of the external side of life. Family, business, health and society form the basis of concern for most people. Now these are all properly the concern of each and every one of us, but not the preponderant concern. Preponderantly our mind should be devoted more to the consideration of the creative principle of life than to its effects and results. If we are in right with the principle we shall not have to worry about results. But the average mind is embroiled in the effect world. At some levels of business in the commercial world the average mind is all day long planning and conniving and juggling and pushing with people and things in order to get results. The mind becomes so involved with process that it forgets the principle of life. Such a mind soon becomes isolated from the central cause of things. In the rough and tumble of the commercial world tensions and vexations are bound to arise and if a mind stays in this world it will fall into the mistake of believing that things are causing other things and events are causing other events, that forces and powers outside of oneself are operating and causing commotion and difficulty. When the mind goes too far in this direction it departs from the spiritual principle of life, the fountain of its energy and its strength. It is dwelling upon the periphery of life and is fast becoming the victim of its circumstances. All of these anxieties and tensions and worries sap the energy of the mind and reduce its efficiency. They have intruded into the holy place where only the presence of God, or serene confidence and peace, should dwell. They are usurping the throne in the sanctuary of God. (Matthew 21:13) The thorns steal the force and fertility of the land, but these cares of this world steal the force and productivity of the mind.

The deceitfulness of riches is a very telling phrase and very descriptive in its four-word simplicity. Some of the other parables will explain it more fully. Just a word here will be sufficient. Lowell expresses it very well:

> For a cap and bells our lives we pay,
> Bubbles we buy with a whole soul's tasking;
> 'Tis heaven alone that is given away,
> 'Tis only God may be had for the asking.
> "The Vision of Sir Launfal"

Thousands of years of recorded history testify to the unreliability of worldly forms of wealth. Every age shows how futile it is to make fame and glory the object of this life. Yet encouragingly enough in every generation there are some, many, in fact, who see that the pursuit of worldly wealth as a means toward security is a dead-end road. They have turned their attention to the pursuit of the treasures of the kingdom. They have seen that to be secure in fortune and in health is to be rich toward God. That means to have confidence and peace and serenity, based upon a clear understanding of the principles which produce these states. Confidence and peace of mind are the only real wealth. They are negotiable in every market of the world. They are readily convertible into any currency of the time and place. The person who has them will never be poor or be in want in terms of the wealth of this world. He, and he alone, is secure. The world's material wealth can never give security to any man, race or institution, hence the deceitfulness of riches.

It is pertinent to include here also that the term riches as Jesus uses it does not mean only silver and gold and property, but riches of the intellect or the mind. Very often people pursue the accumulation of knowledge as though it were a form of real wealth. Then it turns out that they learn many things which aren't so, and their knowledge, instead of a source of security, becomes a source of danger. "He that increaseth knowledge (often) increaseth sorrow." (Ecclesiastes 1:18) There is one kind of knowledge that is without deceit and without sorrow and that is the knowledge of the presence of God in the soul of man. The deceitfulness of riches is the experience of that mind which has occupied itself overmuch with the phenomenal and external side of life and has failed to balance this consideration with frequent contemplation of the wonder and majesty and power of that invisible king who sits upon the throne of the kingdom which is within you. Such a mind is divided in its allegiance, and great portions of its native strength are diverted to the growth of thorns along with its grain. At some point in such a mind's development it will cast out all concept of outside agencies, either benevolent or malevolent, and will give over the field of its mind to the growth of one truth and one only: the fact that consciousness is cause and character is fate, that every desire from the mouth of God in the heart of man carries with it its own mechanics and its own power of fulfillment. In short, that the creative power is in man, that the tabernacle of God is with man, and God dwells there in the heart of man. This makes the mind like a clean field wholly and enthusiastically receptive to the divine seed.

By prayer and meditation the mind may condition itself to be receptive to the highest and the best, to things that are lovely and of good report. Such a mind believes instantly in the infinite possibilities of good. It doubts the prophecies of evil. It is dubious about invisible viruses and dangers and all explanations of phenomena which are not based upon scientific evidence. You cannot easily plant evil suggestions in such a mind. It is geared to good, to confidence, to the affirmation of life. Fears, melancholy, depression, and the predictions of misfortune leave it cold.

The condition of the soil determines the productivity of the seed. Agricultural practice is full of examples of how certain soils are receptive to certain plants and unreceptive to others. Certain plants will not grow on certain soils, the seeds will not germinate. If they do germinate they do not last. Burnt-over timber land in the West produces a beautiful and bountiful crop of fireweed from which the bees gather an excellent honey, but this beautiful fireweed grows only after a fire. The burning of the timber apparently does something to the soil to condition it for the growth of the fireweed. I once burned a pile of oak logs and in the spring the ground produced a beautiful crop of pokeweed nowhere else but on that spot. When the bombs fell upon Britain they stirred up soil which hadn't seen the light of day for hundreds of years. Perhaps the chemicals in the bombs did something to condition the soil, but at any rate flowers which had not been seen for three hundred years in Britain sprouted and bloomed in the rubble. The soil first must be right, and then the seed which falls upon it will be right also and will yield its fullest increase. But it is the soil which is the variable factor, the seed is constant.

But lest we follow too much the point of view that all of this pertains to other people exclusively, let us stop and regard the parable as a mental treatment for our own minds.

That is what the parable is intended to be. It is a transforming agent. It has a healing and an illuminating power
within itself. It is part of that seed with which the sower
sows this world. You must let it fall upon your mind and
allow it to do something to you. Banish the thought that the
parables are stories about other people. They are stories
about you and your mind. Therefore, all of the people in
the parables are not "other people." They are representative of phases and movements of the mind of mankind and
therefore of your mind. Take the parable to yourself and
make it part of you, and it will do things to you. It is so
easy to see indifference and unresponsiveness in another, and
to overlook it in ourselves. It is easy to note the enthusiastic effervescence of a friend who has no staying power,
but it is difficult to detect the same trouble in ourselves.
Yet it is there. All qualities, good and bad, are in every man.
Our individual choices and emphases up to this point have
determined for each of us his character consciousness, personality and experience. What, then, does the parable do to
you when you read it? What does any sacred writing, or
writing of wisdom do to your mind when you hear it or you
read it? Does it move you to faith and assurance, and to
courage? Or does it leave you cold? For, as you are moved,
so you will be moved upon. That is, as you are moved intellectually and emotionally to a new thought or to a new
viewpoint, so experiences and events will move upon you in
confirmation of your inner movement. Now the world is
full of sights and sounds and events which can move you to
tears, to grief, to fear and wild alarm, or to anguish and
depression of spirit, but he who taught in parables said: "Be
of good cheer, I have overcome the world." That is, I have
risen above the place where these sights and sounds and
events can any longer move me.

He who taught in parables calls you to a level of living

where your mind is no longer responsive to the negative things of life, but is open and receptive to the higher truths. It has closed its doors on flesh, and opened them to the spirit. The parables are to help you to accomplish this ascent. The parable is a mover. Read it and ponder it thoughtfully and you will find that its therapeutic magic binds the wounds from which you bleed in this world, and is giving you a transfusion of life from a higher source. So take the parable to yourself and do not be hesitant nor surprised to find within yourself elements of the apathetic, hard-surfaced mind which is cynical or skeptical; which no longer looks forward and upward; which believes that "everything is a racket" and no man is sincere; that life is a battle between pleasure and pain and there is no resolution of the conflict; that man is, as Job long ago said, few of days and full of trouble. Try to see if there is not some negative disposition in your mind which sits like a big, black crow on the garden fence waiting to gobble up the seed that falls upon the ground. Have you wet-blanket propensities? Are you inclined to throw cold water? In other words, are you a believer, not necessarily in some formal confession of faith, but in life and its goodness, its progression and its abundance. Do you believe in your family and your friends? And do you hold the highest concept of the greatest possibility for them? Do you believe in your business and its infinite possibilities? Do you believe that the best things have not happened yet, that the noblest deeds have not been done, that the best inventions have not been made, that the world is young and that opportunity is just now beginning? Do you believe that, as Swedenborg said, the spiritual sun is always shining in the eastern heavens at an angle of forty-five degrees? In other words, that it is always morning?

If you don't, your soil is wayside soil, hard-surfaced and

impacted by the unchecked travel of that throng of limited
concepts, narrow opinions, blind superstitions, anxieties and
fears which treck through the average mind. A productive
soil, as a productive mind, must be loose, pliable, friable.
It must stand the shocks of sudden, heavy rainfall and ab-
sorb them, and it must be able to withstand prolonged
drought. All this a good soil can do. But a poor soil is
quickly eroded by a cloudburst. A hard soil has no capacity
to catch and to hold water, and thus in times of heat and
drought the plants which attempt to grow in it languish
and die. A hardpan beneath the surface of the soil is the
bane of many an agriculturist's life, and he works vigorously
to break it up and to loosen it so that the rain may enter and
the roots of his plants may seek the deeper, mineral-laden
areas of the soil.

Did you ever plant a lawn early in the year, and note
how the grass sprang up and flourished in the wet days of
the early spring? But with the coming of the hot weather
certain areas languished and turned brown. Underneath
these areas was hard ground or rock formations lying impenetrable by rain or root. What ledges of inferiority, guilt,
resentment or prejudice lie buried in many a human mind,
impenetrable by the whisperings of hope and inspiration and
unreceptive to the promises of God and the prophecies of
his prophets! Think about all this and see if you are willing
to let your ground be broken up. See if you are willing to
let old thoughts go and to welcome new ones. Are you bold
enough, brave enough, to put up a no-trespassing sign to
the thoughts of the world which want to think themselves
in you by traversing your ground? Have you courage enough
to believe God who speaks in your own heart, and to disbelieve
the voices of the world? Wouldn't it be wonderful to have
a source of enthusiasm which flows continuously like an
artesian well, rather than to have it come in spurts and jets

which make a great show at first appearance but which gradually peter out and give place to depression and melancholy. Would it not be wonderful to have a source of strength which could not be exhausted by the demands of life's daily tasks and its emergencies. Would it not be an excellent thing for you to have a bank from which you could draw confidence whenever you wished as you would draw money, and so be able to meet every obligation and be able also to buy what you wanted in the market place of life. Those are some of the privileges and prerogatives of good soil and good minds, according to the standard of the spiritual principles of life.

So we come to this great truth, that our ability to receive from others or from life itself, to receive either good or bad, depends entirely upon what we are in ourselves. We have always known that our ability to influence others depends upon what we are. And now we must enlarge our conception to see that what we get and what we give depend upon what we are. All of our life on this planet is getting and giving. To the superficial mind it is the getting and giving of things. To the wise man it is the getting and the giving of consciousness. If we are wise then, we shall work upon ourselves and condition our soil to receive and to respond to the seed of God which is constantly being broadcast upon it. If we have not enough health or strength or love or money or friends, let us know that it is not because of a lack of these things in the universe. Let us look to our soil. Let us develop the soil, and the seeds which are in it will sprout and grow. Cultivate a healthy and vibrant expectancy. Cultivate a love of the beautiful and the constructive. Develop flexibility of mind which admits the sunlight and the rain of heaven to the darker corners of your mind. Imagine yourself as enacting the better and happier roles of life. In other words, condition your mind

with the thought of the highest truths. Then, having made
your soil ready, when the word of God falls upon your soil
it will spring up and bear fruit, some thirtyfold, some sixty,
and some an hundredfold.

THE PARABLE OF THE WHEAT
AND THE TARES

Another parable put he forth unto them, saying, The
   kingdom of heaven is likened unto a man which
   sowed good seed in his field:
   But while men slept, his enemy came and sowed
tares among the wheat, and went his way.
   But when the blade was sprung up, and brought
forth fruit, then appeared the tares also.
   So the servants of the householder came and said
unto him, Sir, didst not thou sow good seed in thy
field? from whence then hath it tares?
   He said unto them, An enemy hath done this.
The servants said unto him, Wilt thou then that we
go and gather them up?
   But he said, Nay; lest while ye gather up the
tares, ye root up also the wheat with them.
   Let both grow together until the harvest: and in
the time of harvest I will say to the reapers, Gather
ye together first the tares, and bind them in bundles
to burn them: but gather the wheat into my barn.
   Then Jesus sent the multitude away, and went into
the house: and his disciples came unto him, saying,
Declare unto us the parable of the tares of the field.
   He answered and said unto them, He that soweth
the good seed is the Son of man;

The field is the world; the good seed are the children of the kingdom; but the tares are the children of the wicked one;

The enemy that sowed them is the devil; the harvest is the end of the world; and the reapers are the angels.

As therefore the tares are gathered and burned in the fire; so shall it be in the end of this world.

The Son of man shall send forth his angels, and they shall gather out of his kingdom all things that offend, and them which do iniquity;

And shall cast them into a furnace of fire: there shall be wailing and gnashing of teeth.

Then shall the righteous shine forth as the sun in the kingdom of their Father. Who hath ears to hear, let him hear.

Matthew 13:24-30, 36-43

IN MARK'S VERSION of the parable of the soils Jesus introduces the parable with the single word: "Hearken!" Then he introduces his interpretation of this parable with the words: "Know ye not this parable? And how then will ye know all parables?" In all three versions of the parable of the soils the Master Teacher uses the expression: "He that hath ears to hear, let him hear." "Take heed," he says, "what ye hear and how ye hear." The emphasis throughout is upon hearing. We have seen that we can hear only something in harmony with what we are. As we hear so we act. As we hear so we see, feel, think, imagine and act. Examples of this principle are all about us in everyday experience. The accents of our daily speech are those we heard in childhood, and unless we work diligently with a speech expert to change them they will not depart from our lips all the days of our life. We have learned our tension and our fears as well as our prejudices and our biases by hearing them and by being exposed to them. In the same way, but with a more constructive result, if we listen to good music for a length of time we develop an ear or an appreciation for it. Paul observes this when he makes that wonderful statement that "faith cometh by hearing." (Romans 10:17) If you have not faith now, frequent the company of those who do have it, and you will find your own ear opening and you, too, will hear the reasons for faith. When you arrive at that strong position of faith where you can command your own thoughts and your own emotions, you are assuming your proper stature and seat of kingship in that kingdom of heaven or spiritual realities toward which all of the parables direct you. There is something special that a man ought to hear in this life.

A man ought to hear the voice of his own soul announcing its regnancy. A man ought to hear that simple majesty within with its still small voice saying: I am and there is none else. (Isaiah 45:5) No casual reading of the parables or even a book of explanation such as this will open the ear to hear that very special announcement. But take heed what ye hear, and read the parables over and over and your ear will open. Start with the sower, and go next to the tares, and you will find a progressive order which will work upon your own mind to hasten the development of the hearing ear. All creative activity moves from the general to the particular, from the universal to the individual. "The great and glorious masterpiece of man," said Montaigne, "is to live to the point." "All judgment," says Jesus, "is committed unto the Son." The cosmic mind has given the individual mind its head, so to speak, in this world. While God stands "within the shadow keeping watch upon his own," he stands there only to advise and to adjust when called upon. And, indeed, to save when the individual mind falters and fails.

The Almighty says to Moses: "I have made thee a God to Pharaoh." The individual mind must learn to accept and to act upon this divine commission. The individual mind has authority over its external world. Not over the world of generalities and universals, but over the world of relationships and particulars concerning itself.

This pattern of things is evidenced in the difference between the first two parables. In the parable of the sower, God, or the cosmic mind, is seen as the sower, sowing the world with the eternal verities or truths of life. Because God is omnipresent his truth is omnipresent. It falls upon every nook and corner of the world. It impinges upon every mind irrespective of the ability of that mind to respond. God is one, but the expressions of God are diverse. In the midst of all the diversity, there is only one. The first parable is concerned with cosmic activity, with generalized action and movement. In the second parable we are concerned with a specialized activity, with the activity of the individual mind in its private world. In his interpretation of the parable Jesus plainly points out: "He that soweth the good seed is the Son of man and the field is the world." The Son of man is the offspring of man. Ordinary thinking conceives of the offspring of man as the issue of his body, but spiritual thinking understands that man is mind. Man's body is his instrument and is not himself except in expression. Man is a generic term, and Son of man means the individual mind with its thoughts and processes. The Son of man in the most ideal sense is exampled in Jesus, the Christ of the Scriptures. Therefore in this second parable we have the individual mind at work in its own particular domain, in its field or vineyard. The parable is concerned with the results the individual mind gets in working in its own field or sphere of interest.

The first parable is concerned about how a man receives

the truth of life in himself, how he receives what God is continually sending him. Each one of us receives some of God's bounty and brings it to maturity in our understanding, whether thirtyfold, sixtyfold, or an hundredfold. What we do with it after that is still another story, and that story is begun in the parable of the tares.

The farmer has to work diligently to keep his field clean of weeds and extraneous growth. He cultivates and harrows and disks incessantly to keep the weeds down. This is like prayer and constructive mental work in our mental and spiritual life. As vagrant seeds carried by birds and by the wind are continually falling upon any piece of ground, so the germs of hate and of grief, defeat, the fears and the tensions and anxieties of men, are passing through the psychic atmosphere in which we live all the time. At any unguarded moment we may pick one of them up and respond unwittingly, and feel in ourselves some fear, some despair, or some piece of gloom, and know no reason for it. Or some other person's negative thinking and prophesying may dampen our spirits, inhibit our industry and enterprise, and generally put the brakes on our energy. On many an occasion you have felt some unreasoning fear, or sense of anxiety, and wondered why, like a spell, it suddenly came over you. The chances are that it floated in and you picked it up, and now you have to cast it off. You have to be as ruthless and diligent with this as the farmer is with his soil. And if you know the principle of the mind, and the principle of cultivating it, you will be vigorous in casting out the dark thoughts, and in renewing your faith and confidence in the goodness of God in the land of the living. Thus, in tending your field, your special area of life, you may indeed plant good seed, images of growth and achievement, of health and happiness. You may have a healthy outlook upon life generally. You may believe in people and trust them, and get along very well with them. But you will be tempted. You will meet what seems like opposition. Perhaps someone in business will be deceitful or faithless with you, to your loss. Then you will be tempted to hate him, or to oppose him as the instrument of your misfortune. Perhaps you have worked hard and given your life for others, either in business or in the family, and because you were or thought you were generous and loyal, you thought that other people were the same. When this proved wrong, your mind may have been tempted to grow bitter, not only at people but at life. All of this and much more is figured in the story of the man who planted his field with good seed, but while men slept, it says, the enemy came and planted tares. Who is the enemy? Surely not another person. The temptation to think so is disastrous. It arouses all the destructive passions of anger and hatred and anxiety. That is why the devil is called the destroyer because he always tempts you into thinking or doing something which will be the means of your own destruction.

The parable says that while men slept the enemy worked evil. While the mind was off guard, while the senses were not diligent, the real enemy, the only enemy there is, belief in limitation, a suggestion of impotency, and intimation of failure, crept in and settled in the mind. Because the mind was asleep, careless, indifferent, it failed to do any mental work to cast out that negative thought and to re-emphasize the mind's positive purpose and goal. Human beings are notorious for taking things easy when everything goes well. We pray feverishly when we get into trouble, but assume there is no need to pray when everything is all right. When the devil is sick he would always be a monk.

The Devil was sick—the Devil a monk would be;
The Devil was well—the Devil a monk was he.

Francois Rabelais, *Works.*

We never know accurately just what the state of our consciousness is until it is brought home to us by our own behavior. Our acts and our experiences are our confirmed thoughts. That is why we have to keep working at our field just as the farmer keeps at his. The "while men slept . . ." in the Parable of the Tares, does not refer to actual sleep at night. It refers to that apathy and dereliction of the mind which assumes that all things will continue to go well even without our mental participation, which neglects to realize that we individually have to keep on the job with our own minds if we would keep our affairs and our health moving along in good fettle. As the pretty and spirited teen-aged girl said when she danced into the living room one evening where her father was reading the paper, and announced joyfully, "Daddy, I am President of our class." "Huh-huh," said her father, hardly looking up from his paper, "how did that happen?" "It didn't happen," replied the young lady. "I happened it." And this is the way it is with most things in our life. We have to get behind our own propositions with our mind if we wish them to succeed.

An old office motto used to stare the visitor in the face: "Who would back you in the race, when defeat is in your face?" Defeat is the seed of the evil one. It is a lie and a falsehood and must not be accepted or tolerated for very long by the intelligent mind. Refuse to go along with the prophets of doom in any event, as Queen Victoria did during some of the dark days of her reign, when she boldly and defiantly announced, "There is no depression in this house." It is while one is asleep to this necessity that the tares are sowed in one's field. Then, because we were asleep we do not know that evil is in us, and therefore we continue blithely and carelessly in our foolish assumption that all is well. If we are diligent in prayer and constructive thinking, however, if we daily work over our minds determining what we really

believe and why we believe it, we shall discover that the
tares are growing there. Then the question is, can you stand
the shock of discovery upon your pride and self-esteem?
Will your ego falter and lose the name of action? Will you
fall into disappointment, despair, self-condemnation and
remorse? The parable says do not oppose the tares. Don't
go out all indignant and excited and try to dig them up, lest
you ruin the positive growth that is also growing in your
field. It is possible to become so exercised, either over a
supposed enemy without or over the real enemy within,
that you destroy more than you intended. If you lose your
peace you lose all. The apostle counsels us: "Resist the
devil and he will flee from you." (James 4:7) But not to
resist evil. In other words, resist the temptation to think
evil or limitation before it actually takes root in your mind,
but once it has actually taken root and grown, don't resist
it, lest you make the field of your mind a battlefield of waste
and destruction.

In other words, this parable is a lesson in how to handle
evil or trouble. Don't get hot under the collar about it. You
don't have to deny it. There it is. If you don't know the
laws of the mind you will be tempted to try and fix the
blame upon some person or some event or series of events
outside of yourself. Then in contemplating this you will get
angry and resentful, and ruin your whole picture by this
emotionalism. Thousands of mature people live daily by the
childish philosophy of "Willie pushed me." It is too over-
whelming a burden to discover that Willie is themselves.
You may have the finest ideas and the best know-how, but
if you indulge in resentment or hate, you will get little yield
from your ideas and your industry. If you admit the law
of the mind, that your experience is the projection of your
own consciousness, and if when the first evidences of your
sowing appear, you discover that it is not one hundred

percent, as you expected it, don't allow disappointment to overwhelm you. And if, in seeking for the cause of the limited results, you find it in your own pride, or anxiety, or fear, or negligence, don't bear down upon it, because you are now identified with it and in fighting it, will hit yourself. Let it alone; this is the lesson of this parable. Let it alone and harvest the good that remains. Out of this particular enterprise, it is true, you will get limited results and that is better than none at all. And having learned a great truth by the whole experience, you will plant again and this time not allow the enemy to work your field while you are unaware. In other words, you will stay on the job with your thought of God and his marvelous omnipotent power in your life, knowing that with this thought you cannot fail, for God giveth increase.

Each person's field, of course, is his own consciousness or mind. He has nothing else to work with except his own thoughts. He has no where else to work except in his own mind among those thoughts. The way to increase the productivity of your field or consciousness, and to increase the amount of seed or truth at the same time, is to work with what you have. If you have only a thirtyfold capacity, put it to work, plant it. It will improve your field. But both the thirtyfold man and the hundredfold man face a common problem, and that problem is another concern of the parable of the tares. This problem has been called the perplexing presence of evil.

To be sure, mankind has always wrestled with the problem of how to account for the evil in the world. If God is the only creator, then he must have created evil also. But this does not sit well, it does not agree with our concept of God as the all-good and as being of too pure eyes to behold evil. Medieval churchmen solved the problem by inventing another creator, the devil, and attributing all evil to him.

But this is in direct conflict with the idea of there being only one God or creator, and this latter is a truth, and not just an idea. It is a mathematical necessity. If there were two creators their wills would clash and there would be no order, no system, no harmony, but rather continual war and chaos. Orthodoxy answers the problem by saying that God permits the devil, or evil, to exist for the tempting and the strengthening of our souls. While there is truth in this, it is actually only a milder way of saying that God creates the evil or at least is responsible for it. A slightly improved version of this theory is to be found in Goethe's *Faust* where God is represented in the prologue as giving the devil temporary permission to tempt man into evil. The great Lord says to Satan: "Divert this mortal from his primal source."

Then there are those who say that evil does not exist, that all is God and his infinite goodness. While there is truth in this also, it quarrels with the common experience of the average man and therefore sets up a conflict within him. The absolute and the relative, the spiritual and the material, are always getting in the way of clear speech and rational understanding. Certainly evil does not subsist, but it does exist. Certainly when war tears our world asunder and millions suffer the most grievous tortures, when misguided men deliberately use falsehood and make falsehood masquerade as truth, when thousands are dying every hour from the most painful diseases, and when, according to a recent report of the F.B.I. there is, in the United States alone a major crime every thirteen and eight-tenths seconds, when the loss of loved ones, of health or of fortune bear down upon all of the race, it is not possible to say that there is no evil experience. But neither does that give us any justification for saying that there is an evil power. Jesus does not teach this. The Bible does not say so. Nor does clear thinking

Eph .6: 12—18

substantiate it, anywhere and at any time. Yet so persistently has such an idea taken hold of the human race that even religious thinkers fight vigorously to sustain it. Thus one divine says, in speaking about the problem of evil: "The sooner men recognize that there is a power in this world which seeks their destruction, the better it will be for them."°

To this writer, such a statement is unfortunate indeed. Take it as a premise for your thinking and reasoning and in spite of all your goodness and righteousness otherwise, you will never be able to deliver yourself from the fear and the spell of evil. By such a premise you have condemned yourself to a fate in accordance with your belief. So long as you postulate an entity independent of yourself, and so long as you cannot bring him out in the open so that you can see and get at him, and have other men see him, you are working and fighting in the dark. You are like a blind-folded man being tormented on every side by enemies who strike and buffet him. He stands up to their blows manfully and courageously and strikes back as best he can, but he is not in control of the situation because he cannot see. His enemies dance nimbly out of his reach and come back to strike him again. The postulates of the human mind are the blueprints of its destiny. They are the credentials for passage into the kingdom of heaven. Or they are the papers that order imprisonment and torture, and perhaps execution itself.

The Bible teaches one uncompromising principle of deliverance, and that is the knowledge that there is only one creative power, that it is neither good nor bad, as men use those relative terms, it is whole and complete in itself. It knows itself and knows no opposition to itself. But where it diversifies and individualizes itself as man it appears at many different levels of awareness or states of mind. These are limited states of mind, and, because they are limited,

° *Studies of the Parables of our Lord,* by Dr. H. T. Sell (Revell).

they see everything through a glass darkly, or they see
things, situations and people only partially. For example,
take the individual who sees the game of life as a deck of
cards stacked against him. This is not true, of course, because in the game of life the cards are always stacked for
you. But this individual thinks that they are stacked against
him. Now, by virtue of the proven law of the mind, that our
mental states are projected into and as our experiences,
this man begins to meet up with troublesome situations and
with difficult people. He mistrusts people so people don't
keep faith with him. He expects trouble, and he finds it
everywhere. He is simply meeting the embodiment of his
mental state everywhere he goes. But because he is ignorant
of this mental law, he has to explain the situation in some
other way. He is unaware of the causes in himself, and since,
he reasons, it is not in himself, it must perforce be outside
and external to him. So he proceeds to look for it. Then he
points the finger at people, to situations, to conditions, and
invents all sorts of forces and powers as the cause of his
difficulty. In many cases one can build up a great deal of
scientific evidence to substantiate the hypothesis of an external cause. But if the scientific method be continued long
enough, and the investigation be wide and thorough enough,
the hypothesis will fall and the single cause as taught in the
Bible will be established. When we do not experience
the presence of God within ourselves, we logically place him
outside and feel apart from him. When we cannot admit
the evil in ourselves, we logically project it and think of
it as something independent of ourselves. Good and evil
are quite relative terms. They describe the relative ways in
which individuals can approach and experience the one life
perfect in itself. There are no absolutes here. One man's
meat is another man's poison. As Sir Richard Burton says
in *The Kasidah*:

There is no Good, there is no Bad; these be the
   whims of mortal will:
What works me weal, that call I "good," what
   harms and hurts I hold as "ill":

They change with place, they shift with race; and,
   in the veriest space of time,
Each Vice has worn a Virtue's crown; all
   Good was banned as Sin or Crime.
                    Sir Richard Burton, *The Kasidah*

The only absolute evil there is, is the denial of the presence
of God, the denial of man's oneness with God, and the
denial of the power of God in man. When you recognize
that there is no evil entity acting independently of man,
but that evil comes from man's mind acting partially, then
you are freed from the thousands of dark fears and superstitions of the unenlightened mind. You take back the power
you formerly gave away and with it you proceed in confidence and assurance to rebuild your life closer to the heart's
desire.

But even then you will not have done with evil, because
the belief in evil is all about us in the world. It is in the
consciousness of the race. Evil is the partial mind, the dark
side of the mind, which, because it is mind, has the power
to project itself into experience. As Dr. Nicoll says, the devil
is the terrible power of misunderstanding. But this terrible
power is abroad in the mind of the race. It gives rise to their
fears, their tensions, their hatreds. Because they do not and
cannot trust themselves, they despoil and persecute other
people. Because they experience limitation and do not know
that that limitation is a projection of their own darkness,
they fear the unknown thing which caused that limitation.
Their griefs and sorrows, their depression and cynicism and

melancholy all pour into the race consciousness like dark streams. You are part of the race so you have to contend with this. Every good and noble thought that you may think may immediately be challenged by some negative and ignoble thought, its opposite. Every yes has its no. Every affirmation has its denial. Every positive affirmation has its negative denunciation. The negative is not a separate force or intelligence. It is simply the denial of the positive force or intelligence. It has its value because against it as with a foil we can see ourselves. By means of it through contrast, we understand the nature of the positive force better. And thus does it help us to grow. As we popularly say, a man learns by his mistakes. In a sense, then, even the devil is not bad, for he helps us, if we understand him correctly, to grow God-ward, just as the zero is a mighty aid in numeration. It is nothing in itself, but when combined with one, we can make ten, or a hundred, or a thousand, and go on multiplying to infinity.

In this sense, then, it is true that God permits the devil to exist and to tempt men. If you think of the devil as negation, or partiality, or misunderstanding, or limitation, then you can readily see how he tempts you. If you see some one with a dreadful sickness and it arouses fear in you that you might have the same thing, then you are being tempted of the devil. This sickness is life in a state of limitation, and it is tempting or pulling upon your mind, suggesting that you image yourself in this fashion. If the actuarial tables of the insurance company say that you have fifteen more years of useful life ahead of you, this is a partial view of life determined by the average man's experience, and the recital of these figures is pulling upon your mind tempting you to think of yourself in terms of the average man's experience. This is limitation and it is devilish. Even though you should fail to achieve anything more than the average man's experience, you should fight against this temptation. "Though he slay me, yet will I trust him." For numerous individuals disprove the actuarial tables in their private experience, as many exceptions to any rule can be found. It is your privilege to think above the suggestions of the sense world and beyond the patterns of racial experience, and above the historical past. As you school yourself in confidence of the one creative power, it will be easier and easier for you to think above the suggested patterns of racial experience and to establish something better in all categories of your life than you otherwise had reason to hope for.

This is the good news of the kingdom of heaven which Jesus brought to earth and which he endeavors to give you to live by in these remarkable stories.

Remember, therefore, that the field is your world, your world of consciousness. The good seed is your positive thought. The bad seed is the negative thought. And the enemy is simply misunderstanding. The harvest is the end of the world. Not the earth or the globe, but the end of your present cycle of consciousness. All things come to an end, and new things are constantly beginning. Your world, at this present moment, is the world of your present thoughts and moods. Whether you are presently enjoying it or not, it is drawing to a close and a new cycle of thoughts and moods will begin. There are cycles within cycles, and worlds within worlds, but we shall study this concept of the end of the world in other parables, so we shall simply conclude here by saying that everything has its period of duration. That is its age, or that is the world. At the end of every experience or piece of work you will total up the good and the bad aspects, burn up the bad in the consuming flames of your newborn insight, and gather the good into the storehouse of your own memory against the day when you will plant again.

THE PARABLE OF THE MUSTARD SEED

Another parable put he forth unto them, saying, The
    kingdom of heaven is like to a grain of mustard
    seed, which a man took, and sowed in his field:
        Which indeed is the least of all seeds: but when it
    is grown, it is the greatest among herbs, and becom-
    eth a tree, so that the birds of the air come and lodge
    in the branches thereof.

                                    Matthew 13:31-32
    *Parallel passages: Mark 4:30-32, and Luke 13:18-
    19.*

THE TRUTH about the mustard seed symbolism is simply
this: that a great and wonderful power is involved in something which by outward appearances is very small and insignificant. The power and the wisdom that are locked up
inside of the mustard seed or any seed for that matter, are
by no means small, weak or insignificant. Our impression
and understanding of a seed is not to be measured by its
appearance. What is outwardly insignificant may be of great
magnitude inwardly. This is the lesson of the mustard seed.
The law of growth and expansion is by means of principles
inside of things, and not by means of facts, qualities and
circumstances on the outside. In truth we learn to judge not
by appearances but to judge righteous judgment as Jesus
says. That is, to judge by the law, the principle of things.
    The mustard seed which we know in the Western world
is not the smallest of seeds, nor is the growth that comes
from it very impressive. The petunia seed far outdoes the
mustard seed in smallness and insignificance. A much more
impressive analogy to anyone on this continent, I would

think, is the redwood tree. In lecturing upon this parable I have often held in my hand a seed of the redwood tree which is found on our western coast. This seed is only a small brown wafer. It looks hardly larger than a piece of tobacco which a smoker might have shaken off the end of a cigarette. It is extremely insignificant outwardly, especially when compared to the thing that comes from it. If this seed were planted, and we could wait around for five to ten thousand years for it to mature into a full-grown tree, we should see a marvel of growth which is unlike anything else upon the face of the earth. Judging by trees which already exist in California, the tree that came from this little brown wafer would reach a height of three hundred and fifty feet—that is a little more than a quarter of the Empire State building. It would measure anywhere from twenty-five to thirty-five feet in diameter. If it were cut down and made into lumber it would take a train several miles long to haul the lumber, and the lumber would build forty-five five-room bungalows. To vary the analogy a little bit, if we were to take this seed and plant it in a tub of earth, carefully weighing the tub and the earth, and then keeping careful account of the weight of the water and the plant nourishment we put into the tub during the years of its growth, and when it reached sizable proportions, weighed the tub and the tree which came from the seed, we should find that we should be unable to account for the weight of the tree in terms of the original earth and the water and the nutriment that we have fed it while it was growing. Where did all this growth come from? We can only answer, out of the air, out of the atmosphere. Some great intelligence working within this tiny wafer of a seed, some magical, mystical, wonderful power involved therein, was able to draw to itself all of the elements necessary to make this marvelous structure of vegetable growth. The redwood tree is indeed "the greatest of herbs." And noting the great bulk, and the height and girth which spring from a little brown wafer such as the redwood seed appears to be, we go down on our knees in worship of the power that is involved in this little thing. That is the lesson of the mustard seed.

The kingdom of heaven is like a mustard seed. The authority of the spiritual mind is like the authority in a seed. The creativeness of the spiritual mind is like the creativeness that is involved within the seed. The Christ mind is like the intelligence and the wisdom which are in the seed. Insignificant and unimpressive outwardly, the Christ man is nevertheless the strongest and the best kind of mind among men. Mind doesn't usually impress men as much as matter does. And therefore to say that mind is a power, a ruler, an authority, a kingdom, is foolish talk to those minds which are impressed by the forms and shapes and movements of material things. And for that reason Isaiah, the prophet, says of Him:

> . . . he hath no form nor comeliness; and when we shall see him, there is no beauty that we should desire him. He is despised and rejected of men; a man of sorrows, and acquainted with grief: and we hid as it were our faces from him; he was despised, and we esteemed him not.
>
> Isaiah 53:2-3

Thousands pay pious tribute to an historical Christ, the object of their projected awe and worship, and even love. But who, as Isaiah asks, "hath believed our report, and to whom is the arm of the Lord revealed?" Who believes in the authority of that Christ immanent in his own nature? Paul says: "Christ in you, the hope of glory," to the Colossians, saying further that this is the mystery which hath been hid from ages and from generations, but now is made manifest to his saints. (Colossians 1:26-27) Christ *is in man*

natively and inherently, not outwardly and obviously and
functionally. But Christ is in man inherently in the same
way that an oak tree is within the acorn, and a mustard
bush is within the mustard seed. Have faith in this, for it is a
great wisdom and power always available to you. Having
faith in this is having faith in yourself in the truest sense.
"The kingdom of heaven is within you." What is this kingdom of heaven that is within you? The power and the wisdom to do and to be and to have all that is necessary, all that
is needful in the life of man. The announcement of this and
its understanding is the message of the Gospel, for it is the
good news of the kingdom of God.

When Jesus came down off the Mount of Transfiguration,
there came to him a man who had a lunatic son. The man
kneeled down and pleaded with Jesus to heal his son:

Lord, have mercy on my son: for he is lunatick, and sore
vexed: for ofttimes he falleth into the fire, and oft into the
water.

And I brought him to thy disciples, and they could not cure
him.

Then Jesus answered and said, O faithless and perverse
generation, how long shall I be with you? how long shall I
suffer you? bring him hither to me.

And Jesus rebuked the devil; and he departed out of him:
and the child was cured from that very hour.

Then came the disciples to Jesus apart, and said, Why could
not we cast him out?

And Jesus said unto them, Because of your unbelief: for
verily I say unto you, If ye have faith as a grain of mustard
seed, ye shall say unto this mountain, Remove hence to
yonder place; and it shall remove; and nothing shall be impossible unto you.

Matthew 17:15-20

If there is any one case more difficult than another to heal it is the case of insanity, for an insane person has given up his reasoning powers and has retreated from the daylight of life into the shadows of his own unconscious wishes and frustrations. He is a dead weight for the healer to carry because he is unable to do anything for himself. In the case of an ordinary neurotic mind there is enough sense of reality left to enable the person to recognize his problem and want to solve it. The mind can still reason and think and it will usually cooperate with the healer to help itself. This is also true of injury to the human body. If a person has been in an accident and physically injured, but not too seriously, you can usually give him a "fireman's lift" and get him out of danger and into a place of safety. That means you help him to get on his feet and you bear part of his weight until he can walk alone. If he has been injured to the point of total immobility, however, he cannot move by himself alone. Therefore you must lift his whole weight by yourself. It is like this in mental healing. A healer who can get no cooperation from the conscious mind whatever must bear the total "weight" of the sick person psychically. We bear one another's burdens whenever we undertake to show the truth to one another. It calls for great clarity and strength of thought. And in this Bible reference we have the case of the disciples failing in this regard, whereas the Master succeeds. In explaining their failure to the disciples Jesus points out that their faith was imperfect. He upbraids them for their unbelief. He does not say weakly that God didn't want you to have an answer to this prayer, or God didn't want to heal the lunatic and that is why your prayers were not answered. He states it plainly and categorically that the reason for their failure was "your unbelief."

This is the simple truth of all such situations: if thoughts are things actually, not merely in theory and philosophy, if

mind is matter, if consciousness is fate and experience, if all
thinking is incipient action, then when we fail to demonstrate our thought it is plain that we did not have the
thought we thought we had. There should be no attempt
at escape from the straight track of this principle because
there is no escape in logic or science. All attempts at escape
lead to delusion and loss of faith. Real faith is the conviction
that the creative presence is active in every thought of the
mind. More or less faith is not a question of quantity, but
rather of quality and clarity of perception. The disciples
had a little faith. They believed in their teacher. They gave
mental assent to his philosophy. They believed that miracles
could be done because they had seen him do them. In
many cases they had done them themselves. But when it
came to the lunatic, their senses were overwhelmed by the
sights and the sounds of this formidable malady of unconscious control. This certainly looked like the action of
another power and their perception of the one power waned.
The moment your mind admits another power, you give
hostages to fortune and thereby weaken your bargaining
position from then on. Admission of another power requires
that you oppose and resist the power. This puts the mind in
that impossible position of creating and fighting its own
belief. This is confusion, irrationality and weakness. The
word of such a mind no longer has power. It has consumed
its power in its own conflict. It may petition a theoretical
God of mercy for help but actually it denies the God of
mercy by its belief in a power of evil, and so it gets no help
from its prayer of petition.

It takes the Master consciousness which has just descended
from communion and identification with the divine to heal
the lunatic. It takes that kind of consciousness which is so
identified with universals that it is unconcerned with par-

ticulars. To such a mind the facts of a situation neither
depress nor stimulate. Its strength and its elevation come
from consideration of the principle of life rather than the
appearance of life. Such a mind's whole mode of thinking
and action is based upon the rule: "Judge not according to
appearances but judge righteous judgment (according to
principle)." Such a mind maintains its independence of facts
and circumstances and its leverage over them. Ordinary
minds judge by appearances and that is why they often
mistake the lesson of the mustard seed. The ordinary mind
is impressed by the sensations that come to it through the
outer senses. Size, loudness, color, keenness and intensity
of feeling of sensation, all impress the ordinary mind very
strongly. They arouse its attention and cause it to wonder
and admire and to stand in awe of the source of its sensations. Hollywood indulges in extravaganzas, riots of sound
and color and movement, to impress its customers. The
military has always used stirring music and colorful uniforms
to establish its identity in the minds of people.

But the thoughtful theater-goer gets tired of the empty,
plotless, thoughtless, themeless shows, and longs to have
mummers portray life for him, to activate his inner senses
with the strengthening and enduring values of life. And
the statesman who is truly concerned with the safety and
perfection of his country does not think with the emotions
of the crowd, emotions which the crowd has when the bugles
and uniforms go marching by. He is rather concerned with
the integrity and loyalty of men in government, with industry and productiveness, with planning and farsighted-
ness, which alone are the protection of a country in peace
and in war. When we are very young we are naturally
devoted more to the facts and sensations of life than to the
principles which are behind them as causes. To a boy or

girl in college, clothes, for example, are a very important
item. As one young teen-ager said: "One might as well be
dead as not have the right clothes to wear." With the coming of maturity we are much more impressed by a knight
in the shining armor of a blue serge suit than a knave in
evening dress of the latest style and cut. The sensualist is
concerned with how things titillate his taste buds and the
olfactory nerves. The materialist is impressed with the
thought that money can buy anything, or that science can
make or cure anything. The materialist puts his trust in
houses and lands, and is unimpressed with the treasures that
are in heaven. He relies on miracle drugs and upon new
techniques to give him health. Then when misfortune or
illness comes he is impressed by the symptoms and suffer-
ings as the signs and wonders of an evil power trying to
destroy him. He is without faith because he has never
thought about that which makes faith. He is weak because
he has no faith. Being so long impressed by, and so overwhelmed by the impressions of, size and form and shape
and color and tangibility, there is no awareness in such a
mind of the mighty power of intangibles.

And this, too, is the lesson of the mustard seed. It is "the
smallest of seeds," but what a job it does, what an impression it makes when it is full grown! Many people have
erroneously supposed that since the mustard seed is "the
smallest of seeds" and since it is used by Jesus as the symbol
of faith, then all that they need is a little faith. Nothing
could be farther from the truth. A little faith goes a little
way, as a little of anything goes a little way. A little faith
gets a little money, a little health and a little happiness.
Probably nowhere so much as in matters of religion and faith
do people expect so much from so little. In every other field
it is plain that we get out of something exactly what we put

into it, that the law of action and reaction is operative in the world. Yet in matters of faith we come to the easy conclusion we can get something for nothing, that we can get a blessing from the Almighty without understanding his ways and his laws and the principles by which he operates. We do not get something for nothing, and neither does the mustard seed. The idea that a small, weak, insignificant little thing will draw a great reward out of heaven is misleading, to say the least. The power of heaven is right there, within the seed itself.

There is involved within you, as well, a miracle of power and wisdom and intelligence, not only similar to, but greater than that contained within the mustard seed. To believe fully and adequately in this is probably the hardest thing we, as human beings, ever find to do. It is easy to have faith in other people, and in things and in processes and in mechanical methods of operation. It is difficult to find a reason for faith in oneself. People have faith in everything but themselves. How then can you have faith in yourself? By remembering that you are a seed of divinity, that all the powers of the God-head are rolled up in your soul, as the greatness of the tree is rolled up within the seed. As the mighty redwood is involved in this little brown wafer; as the great mustard shrub of the East is involved in the little mustard seed; and indeed, as any plant, humble or great, is involved within its seed; so God is involved within you, and the whole process of your life is the evolution of that which has been planted within you. You are not to judge solely by your outward appearance, or by your outward history, or by your outer description or by other people's viewpoints or descriptions of you. All men have this in common, that God indwells them. That all they will ever be or all they will ever need is now within them, awaiting that proper soil which will allow the inside potential to manifest itself.

The first parable showed us the importance of getting the soil of our mind ready to be a true host to the seed which has already fallen upon us. The second parable showed us the importance of distinguishing between the true and the false, which has also fallen upon us, and not to fight or resist it while it was present with us. And now this third parable about the seed impresses upon us the truth of "the infinitude of the little." It tells us not to be impressed by things that look beautiful but are not, that seem powerful but are not, which come like the idiot's tale full of sound and fury, signifying nothing. We are reminded to reserve our highest awe, worship and praise for the still small voice, and for that invisible presence and wisdom in all of life, including ourselves. Though outwardly insignificant, it is inwardly and truly the most formidable and significant thing in all the world. Its tremendous force and power can find no better example than the amazing example of a tiny little seed expanding from within and becoming a tree in which the birds come to make their nests.

The parable shows us, too, how to relieve ourselves of the sense of effortfulness and burden. For it implies that our effort consists in getting the soil of our own mind's receptiveness in good condition, and then allowing the seed to take over the work. Man's labor is to see the truth. From that point on the truth works upon man and in him.

THE PARABLE OF
THE SEED GROWING SECRETLY

And he said, So is the kingdom of God, as if a man should cast seed into the ground;

And should sleep, and rise night and day, and the seed should spring and grow up, he knoweth not how.

For the earth bringeth forth fruit of herself; first the blade, then the ear, after that the full corn in the ear.

But when the fruit is brought forth, immediately he putteth in the sickle, because the harvest is come.

Mark 4:26-29

THIS PARABLE is found only in Mark and therefore is not properly a part of the Sermon by the Sea, but because of its subject matter it belongs with the other parables about seeds. It has a particular and peculiar emphasis of its own, namely the wisdom and the power, the wonder and the magic of the miracle of creation as it unfolds from a seed. What is more powerful or more dominant than seed? It is in the earth, it fills the earth, and it is always growing and changing the earth. Destroy all the visible seeds of a certain plant species and there would still be some left in the earth beneath the levels of heat and light which cause germination, and when the time was right and the soil was stirred those seeds would germinate and burst into growth. Some seeds retain their viability for thousands of years. Some seeds which were found in King Tutankhamen's tomb sprouted and grew after being buried for centuries.

What is a seed? A seed is an organized potential. A seed

is self-sufficient. It has its own life within itself. It can
grow by itself. It has its own mechanics and its own mathematics within it. The seed has the power of self-movement.
Where conditions of light and moisture and heat are not
right, it will remain inactive. Where these conditions are
right, it will put forth first the blade, then the ear, then
the full grain in the ear. This parable calls particular attention to those movements and activities which take place on
the invisible side of life and which man too often and too
easily forgets. The activity of life is not confined to the surface and to externals, to the land of the senses. There is
activity in the ground where myriads of bacteria swarm.
There is activity in the air, and in the interstellar spaces.
There is activity in man's unconscious which he is not consciously aware of. There is an invisible something in the
seed which determines its growth and progress. There is
an invisible force in man which determines his growth and
progress. More particularly speaking, there is an unconscious and invisible side to you as an individual. This unconscious side must be reckoned with.

You don't throw seeds around idly and carelessly upon
the surface of the earth. You might then reap a sturdy and
formidable growth where you wanted a delicate blossom.
Similarly, you must not throw ideas around carelessly because your subconscious is the ground which catches them
and does something with them. The subconscious is as responsive to ideas as the ground is to seeds. Therefore Jesus
points out that a man shall give account in the day of judgment for every idle word. From a mental science point of
view the judgment is merely the end of a mind cycle. For
example, the idea for the Parsifal drama came to Richard
Wagner in 1862. He responded to the idea and took it into
his own subconscious ground where it worked underground,
so to speak, for twenty years. When this subconscious ac-

tivity was finished it projected itself into Wagner's conscious mind and he went to work on it and completed it. Everything which impresses us leaves a seed with us. That seed grows up and becomes an attitude or a tendency or an action. Sometimes we fail to solve a problem or to meet an issue squarely and decisively when it first confronts us. Through fear or sloth we put it off and it is submerged into the subconscious where it continues to live and to move, finally to confront us again in a far stronger form than before. The judgment time is the harvest time and the mind reaps the fruit of its constructive attitudes and acknowledges the results of its destructive concepts. What the mind could not refuse as an idea must now be accepted as a fact and an experience and understood. A connection must be made between the experience and the thought, and then the mind comes to judgment and to discretion. All goes to show that there is an activity in the subconscious side of our life which we cannot ignore. It enters into everything we do and are.

All real learning must center around the knowledge that there are three parts to the life process: planting, growth and harvest. We are proud of our scientific knowledge, but when you survey it critically, we know so very, very little. What do we actually know of the growth of the seed in the ground? Man deals with planting and harvesting, and man can understand these. The middle part is always a mystery. The farmer plants and the farmer harvests, but God giveth the increase. How the seed which the farmer plants expands from within itself, grows, reaches out and procures food is not a part of human knowledge. Between planting and harvesting there is a mystery. Between every beginning and every ending, in any function or process which you choose to mention, the middle portion is not the subject of scientific research or philosophic description. We simply know nothing about it. We are justly proud of man's knowledge, but actually he knows so very little. "The philosophy of six thousand years," says Emerson, "has not searched the chambers and magazines of the soul." * Man knows how to plant and he knows how to harvest, but beyond affording the conditions to help it grow better, man does not know how to make a seed grow. Yet were it not for the seed and the way of the seed in the ground, man would perish before the next harvest. Today we know a lot about how the chemical elements have an affinity for one another and join and combine to form many different products. The very clothes on our backs today fashioned by chemistry are dramatic and thrilling proof of this knowledge. And we know a great deal today too about the behavior of the atom and its component parts. What the ancient alchemists dreamed of doing, modern science can now accomplish, that is, turn one element into another by changing the composition of the atom. But this again is only planting and harvesting. It is dealing with beginnings and with ends.

To the ancient people the fermentation of juices in the absence of yeast appeared to be spontaneous, and they attributed it to a spirit or spirits. Then about the time when beet sugar first was made, Lavoisier, father of modern chemistry, suggested that the essence of fermentation was in the decomposition of sugar. But now that we know the peculiar behavior of the carbon and the mathematical precision of all the chemical elements, have we utterly destroyed the spirit or the unknown agency that is working behind and in and through all things? Isn't there still a mystery left in it all? Is there not still some unexplained miracle between the crushing of a fruit and the distillation of alcohol from it? The very law of affinity by which all of these processes take place is a mystery and a miracle in itself. The law explains how something is being done,

* *The Oversoul* by Ralph Waldo Emerson.

but it doesn't explain what is being done. We know how to set up conditions in order to achieve a certain end, but the actual achievement belongs to an agency other than man. Call it the law of affinity, or nature, or spirit, or what you will.

Every function, therefore, has its three stages. The beginning and the end are man's, the middle belongs to God. The parable of the seed growing secretly is designed to impress this truth upon us. The seed is the very best illustration of this truth. But the purpose of the parable is to show us what our own minds are like. For it is a kingdom of heaven parable, and plainly says that the kingdom of heaven is like the seed growing secretly.

As in agriculture so in the development of the human mind and of the kingdom of heaven within that mind. Ideas are seeds and every idea is incipient action; every idea is a promise and a prophecy. The idea contains within itself the power of realization and movement. No more practical principle can be known and realized by the human mind than this. This is the fundamental principle of mental science and of all spiritual therapeutics. It is the essential and basic teaching of the Bible and of every parable. Not only the great spiritual thinkers of the race, but scientific researchers into the laws of mind have found this principle to be the mind's basic structure.

In the beginning of the nineteenth century Phineas Quimby, experimenting with the mind and perfecting his practice of healing by the mind alone, stated it this way: "I found that if I really believed a thing the effect would follow whether I was thinking of it or not." And in the last part of that century and the first part of this, Professor Bernheim of the Nancy School in France discovered the same thing and worded it this way: "Every idea is action in a nascent state." Every idea accepted by the brain tends to corresponding action, every cerebral cell energized by an idea energizes in its turn the nerve fibers which are to realize this idea. Thus thought is act in the nascent stage. Thought is the beginning of activity. "The idea," said Professor Bernheim, one of the early psychotherapists, "becomes sensation or movement." There is no thought without expression. There is no prayer without its fulfillment. Every idea is a seed of action and experience, and if you think the idea, it falls upon the sensitive medium of your mind just as seed falls upon the ground, and it springs up, first the blade, then the ear, then the full grain. You do not cause the idea to grow. The idea has an action within itself. You have only to think the idea vividly and let it go to work in good soil, with proper care, in order for it to reproduce itself in form and, finally, to function. (I will speak further about the transformation of idea into practical action in the discussion of the next parable.) What immense possibilities loom before us when we know this! What dark citadels of fear fall and crumble away at the remembrance of this principle! How beautiful upon the mountains are the feet of him who brings us these tidings, that in our own thought is the key to all our living and experience. There is no evil agency to fear as being opposed to our good.

If you personally perceive this principle clearly, then you have faith as a seed. Recall that it was said, "If you have faith as a grain of mustard seed, nothing is impossible unto you." Why? Because you recognize a potential within yourself which, in regard to your pursuits and concerns, is almighty and all-wise, and is self-moving. Notice that it says that if you have faith *as* a grain of mustard seed, not the faith *of* a mustard seed. The mustard seed, being a seed, is, as we have seen, self-moving, having the capacity of growth within itself. If you recognize this principle as true of yourself, that is, that you have the principle of initiation and growth and movement toward your ideals within yourself, then you have faith as a mustard seed or as any seed. The result of knowing this is that nothing is impossible unto you. Your awareness is your faith, and with this new awareness you can no longer be negative and fearful, you can no longer give power to externals, you no longer postulate enemies and antagonists and blocks and oppositions outside of the self. Since all of this is true therefore all things are possible unto you. What was not possible to you before, is now possible, not because you have increased in strength and can therefore force a result by throwing your weight around, but whereas before you faced dead-ends and formidable barriers, now you can see your way clear upon the basis of this fundamental principle of planting and harvesting. Things are possible with this awareness. This awareness is faith. And faith is a seed which carries the potency of life from one generation or expression of life to the next.

THE PARABLE OF THE LEAVEN

Another parable spake he unto them; The kingdom of heaven is like unto leaven, which a woman took, and hid in three measures of meal, till the whole was leavened.

Matthew 13:33

Parallel passage in Luke 13:20–21.

WE HAVE THUS FAR been dealing with seeds for planting in the soil. Now we shall deal with seeds that are ground, or with the meal or flour which is obtained by crushing the seeds. And this will bring us one step closer to understanding ourselves and will help each of us to lay hold upon his own greater powers for good. Seeds are truths. In the Parable of the Sower we saw that the universal mind scatters these seeds over all of the earth, and they germinate and spring up and flourish in various degrees according to the soil upon which they fall. In the parables of the tares and the mustard seed and the seed growing secretly we saw how man apprehends the universal truths, takes hold of them, and deliberately plants them in the earth of his own mind for increase of perception and understanding. But this is not enough. It is not only the increase of ideas which we want. Rather we want to make use of the ideas to increase our sense of life and happiness. The Parable of the Leaven tells us that we must do something with the seed, something more than mere planting of it. The planting of one seed will give us a plant which has more seeds, and we shall have many. But after a time we must do more than merely increase the number of our seeds. We must take them and crush them into flour, mix the flour with leavening which will cause it to rise and to expand. And then, finally, though the parable does not specifically carry us this far in thought, we must eat the product and further transform the seed into the life of man, flesh and blood and brain and thought and feeling.

It is obvious that in this world what counts is the practical kind of action that gets results. Ideas must always be transformed into action. That man who asked the woman with the crying baby if her child had been christened yet, and if it had not, he would suggest the name "Good Idea" because it needed carrying out, was only making a wise crack about an old and obvious truth. As our popular language has it, "ideas are a dime a dozen." Theories and schemes and plans abound. Hopes and dreams and good intentions are abundant. But for every ten people who have good ideas there is probably only one who has the developed ability of turning ideas into actions. For these latter people the world reserves its biggest rewards. They are constantly in demand. The world never has enough of them. They have received the universal truths and have thought about them. They have planted and harvested and increased their number. The next step, as the present parable suggests, is to take some of that increase and crush it into meal, leaven it and eat it, that it may become flesh and blood and thought—in short, action and movement. Someone might say, well, it was movement before when it was a growing plant. Yes, but now it is a different kind of movement. It is human movement, outward action.

Change or transformation simply means a different movement. All life is made of one stuff. Basically, life consists of energy or spirit which is always moving, in and as one form or another. An idea is a moving thing in the intellectual sphere. The action of an idea is the same energy moving physically. Jesus points out elsewhere that this change from intellectual to physical action is necessary. "Except a corn of wheat fall into the ground and die, it abideth alone: but if it die, it bringeth forth much fruit." (John 12:24) Any seed which you plant in the ground, be it a kernel of wheat or a piece of potato, dies in the ground, and in dying bequeaths its energy to new forms of itself. The analogy of this with the human mind and its principles and functions is quite exact. The reader must not forget at this point that we are still dealing with the kingdom of heaven, we are still with Jesus by the seaside where he is instructing the people in the nature of the kingdom of heaven, and saying in each parable: "The kingdom of heaven is like . . ." Thus a man who has a brilliant idea must die as a theorist in order to become a practicer. The dreamer must die that the doer may be born. If you deal with an idea long enough, that is, meditate upon it and think about it and around it, you will notice that the action soon reverses itself. Instead of your dealing with an idea, the idea is now dealing with you. The polarity has changed, and instead of the action beginning with you and impinging upon the idea, the action is now taking place in the idea and it is moving you, and animating you. In this principle is the true science of the mind. "Nature obeys us as we first obey nature." Every man in the last analysis must approach an idea as a suppliant and a servant. If he does his service well in meditation and realization, the idea will in turn exalt him and set him on high, and with long life satisfy him and show him salvation. (Psalm 91)

Working with an idea in this fashion has been called "getting it into one's blood." And thus the analogy with seed and flower that comes from it is apt. How do we get the life of the seed into our bodies? Literally, by crushing it and causing it to die as a seed and be transformed into meal or flour. Then we put yeast or leavening into it to cause it to rise. This gives it flavor and palatability. Then we eat it. What happens? The elemental vegetable life of the seed becomes our life by the mysterious and wondrous metabolism and blood chemistry of the human body. One kind of life is transformed into another and higher kind. That slice of toast you ate for breakfast, for example, was made from the wheat of the field. It was leavened and raised into a loaf. You ate that bread and now, after a few hours, it is your flesh and blood. The life of the wheat was one thing. The life of a human being is another. There are, as Paul points out, different kinds of flesh, and that life which was once wheat and now is flesh and blood is not just ordinary or average human flesh and blood. It is a particular kind of human life because you are a particular kind of individual and because the life of the wheat is now the life of your blood, and because the life of the blood is the life of the brain and its thinking process, your very thought may be said to be the transformed life of the wheat. This, by the way, is essentially the doctrine of transubstantiation, once you remove it from its ecclesiastical trappings. °

How does all this wondrous and magical transformation take place? We do not know all about it, either in the physical, bodily process, or in the metaphysical, mental process, which are here considered together in this parable, as parallel processes. We don't know exactly how the bodily wisdom transforms the life of the wheat germ into the life of the blood cell. We do know, however, that this process is modified by the individuality of the person concerned. We do know that whether or not this bodily process builds health or not is determined by the individual consciousness, which means the person's beliefs and moods. We know that to get something into our consciousness or "into our blood," to speak figuratively, we have to qualify it and impregnate it with feeling. Ideas of themselves have no motion until we give them motion. Ideas are static until the mind of man gives them his own dynamic. If you want something very much and your mind can consider it positively and confidently, you will bring the warmth of life or feeling to the idea, and this will unlock the life in the idea and cause it to flow into and blend with your own. This amounts to nothing more than feeling or animation or enthusiasm, which will direct and guide and compel you into the enactment of the role suggested by the idea. It is feeling, then, that transforms ideas into action. It is enthusiasm, animation and the will to act which make the difference between the dreamer and the doer. There are thus three parts to any process of transforming an idea into action. There is the idea itself, there is the feeling and then the act. And that is why the number three is prominent in the parable of the leaven.

° *See my The Great Prayer,* p. 4.

There are three measures of meal, or three divisions of the life process.

In the previous parables of the seeds we were dealing with men. Now we are dealing with a woman. And this is not alone in observance of the fact that men usually do the planting and the harvesting, and women do the baking and the cooking, or that man's work is with the seed, and woman's work with the flour which comes from the seed. But this is in observance of the fact that man represents thought and woman represents feeling. This is not to say that man is all intellect and woman is all feeling, or that man reasons better and woman is more proficient with intuition. Both functions are in both men and women. The division of the sexes physically is only representative of the two functions of metaphysical or spiritual man. The feeling nature of each person is a woman or the "womb-man," and it is this part of us which must take and handle the crushed seed, give it the leavening or the rising and expanding qualities, and transform it into form and function. So the parable says that it was a woman who did the work. The kingdom of heaven is like the leaven which she hid in three measures of meal until the whole was leavened.

In the first four parables, the kingdom of heaven has been likened unto seeds which the mind apprehended, handled, planted and increased in the harvest. This is the work of the mind, or male part, the intellectualizing and reasoning faculty. It deals with ideas and perceptions. It multiplies and increases its understanding through analysis and meditation. But all the grain in all the granaries of the world would be of little use unless made into flour and bread, so that bread in turn could become flesh and blood. So the heart must take over what the mind has prepared. From the field and the granary and the mill, the life, which is the wheat, must go to the house and to the woman. The woman can do something to the meal which will prepare it for another kind of life. She can hide leavening within it. She can infuse her spirit into it. She can put feeling and animation and enthusiasm all through it, until it has a self-acting quality, until it expands and grows beyond its present measure, until it spreads into all three measures of thought, feeling and action. Our English word "enthusiasm" comes from Greek words which mean "possessed by the God."

God is spirit, and spirit is animation or feeling. When you are inspirited you are possessed by a feeling and an animation and an enthusiasm which is thorough; just as the meal is possessed by the leaven. This animation is the action of the only power there is, the spiritual power. Being alone, it has no opposite. Having no opposite, it has no antagonist or opposition. Therefore it accomplishes that whereunto it is sent and directed. You can acquire this enthusiasm or possession by the spirit in regard to your good purposes and desires in life by remembering the simple law that "thoughts are things." Grant the creative law of your own thought power of your own thought, and you are at once delivered from all reason for discouragement or hopelessness and are inspired by a little bit of leaven which shall very quickly spread to all three measures of your meal and deliver you from your present position into a higher level of experience and happiness.

THE PARABLE OF THE HIDDEN TREASURE

Again, the kingdom of heaven is like unto treasure hid in a field; the which when a man hath found, he hideth, and for joy thereof goeth and selleth all that he hath, and buyeth that field.

Matthew 13:44

THE PARABLE OF
THE PEARL OF GREAT PRICE

Again, the kingdom of heaven is like unto a merchant
man, seeking goodly pearls:
    Who, when he had found one pearl of great price,
went and sold all that he had, and bought it.
                                    Matthew 13:45-46

THESE TWO, and the following parable, are all lessons in discrimination and selection. A sense of values is the most
important development in anyone's life. Knowing the true
from the counterfeit, the superior from the inferior, is the
business of everyone of us whatever his field or occupation.
Look at the piece of paper upon which these words are
printed. To you there may not be any difference in one side
from the other. But to the experienced eye of a printer or a
paper manufacturer, there is a marked difference. In a page
of book paper such as this is, the difference is inconsequen-
tial because we use both sides. But in a piece of fine bond
paper that difference increases in importance and determines
the right side from the wrong side. You and I may not readily
know a piece of good money from a piece of bad, but the
bank teller knows at a glance. A tailor knows his cloth,
whether in the bolt or on the back. The butcher knows his
meat, whether on the hoof or on the block. And the execu-
tive at the corner bank in charge of loans knows the value
of your house and mine. Successful business men are notorious for their shrewdness in judging and predicting values. The ability to judge values is most evident in the
business world. The simplest mind in dealing with the com-
modities of the physical world can develop a keen sense of
shrewdness and discrimination.

It is not odd, therefore, that these first two parables relate to business and the commercial value of property, and in pursuing our knowledge of the kingdom of heaven, or our awareness of that government which is our own conscious-ness, we must remember that this principle of discrimina-tion between the lesser and the greater extends upward infinitely. The kingdom of heaven is within, so a man must learn to be a good merchant inside, with his thoughts and his feelings. He must learn to be a shrewd observer of him-self and his works and to know a treasure when he sees it. Russell Conwell, in his famous *Acres of Diamonds,* brought the idea home forcibly to millions of hearers and readers. He told of the Pennsylvania farmer who grew tired and discour-aged with the failure of his farming operation and moved to Ontario in search of the fabled riches of new land. The new owner of the Pennsylvania farm took his stock to water and noticed an oil slick on the surface of the creek. This led to the discovery of the famous Pennsylvania oil.

Riches are all about us if we could but see. They are all through us, inside and out, if we could but understand. This is the meaning of the Parable of the Hidden Treasure. Every man can have the treasure if he knows how to seek for it within himself. Every person, therefore, is the field in which the buried treasure lies. But this is not always easy to understand. For years and years our minds have been too easily impressed with the "buried treasure" aspects of this parable. Commentators are fond of pointing out that in ancient Biblical times there were no banks and therefore the practice of burying one's savings was very common. A man might bury his money in a certain corner of his field and then die without revealing the secret. Years later a tenant, or a neighbor, or an itinerant, or a villager out for a walk, or any other non-owner of the farm might stumble upon the evidences of the treasure. Obviously, a shrewd man would hide all evidence of his find, and if the treasure was greater than his present holdings he would proceed to liquidate all his present holdings and get enough cash to buy that field. He would give up the lesser for the greater.

But too often the inference is drawn that the kingdom of heaven is a treasure which you just stumble upon without any previous design or preparation, and the result is a sort of windfall. The parable can bear this interpretation up to a point, but not too far. There is, indeed, a buried treasure in each and every human being. His potentialities are enormous. His possibilities are infinite. He is peculiarly equipped and geared to do everything that he can ever desire to do, and to do it grandly. But he will never come upon that treasure without work within and upon himself, to change his own consciousness about everything. With any buried treasure you have to dig in order to get it out. There is some effort involved. But this is not all. Before you are granted the right to dig in the field where you have discovered the buried treasure, you have to own that field, and most men do not own their own minds. You have to sell what you have, and liquidate your holdings, and with the cash buy that field; then you have the right to dig. All this requires a bit of doing. And this is what a great many people shy away from. They would much rather that the universe honor their good intentions as legal tender for their debts and for their purchases. They would rather somebody else go bond for them and do the work for them, in the mistaken belief that they can realize the kingdom of heaven within themselves in this fashion. And thus many a Christian finds it easy to accept what he thinks is the doctrine of vicarious atonement which offers the opinion that one historical God-man ransomed us all by his death, and that all we have to do is to believe this and all will be well. But all is not well even with those who say they believe, because their belief is in a

shadow and a misapprehension of the real thing. The Christ
man or saviour is involved in every son of man, but he is
submerged in an unconscious state and the sense-mind, conscious and dominant, overrules him. When these positions
are reversed and the Christ-mind has died to unconscious-
ness and is resurrected into consciousness, then all mistakes
and sins and shortcomings are done away with in one fell
swoop. It is psychological change and spiritual awakening
that are necessary to change a man and his experience.

Thus you have to change within yourself, in your thoughts
and your feelings and your attitudes and your outlook, about
yourself and other people and all things. You have to give
up what you now hold in exchange for what you want. How
can you believe in the creative law of your own mind while
you also try to hold to the belief that other people and conditions in general are making or marring your life? This is a
contradiction and an impasse, with the prize going to
neither side. The kingdom of heaven is a new kind of mind,
and it can be established only by turning over the old kind
of mind. It is the belief of the sense-bound mind that externals are the causes and the conditioners of our life and
our experience. Upon this premise arise all our resentments
and hates and anxieties and depressions. Only when we accept the principle of spiritual causation can we destroy this
whole brood of dark thoughts and emotions. Any mind
which studies these things will soon be led to see that many
of its concepts and opinions and attitudes are untenable in
the light of the law that "thoughts are things." The belief
that another can possibly be your enemy, the belief that you
are the football of chance, the belief that you must struggle
and fight and oppose powers and conditions outside of yourself—all these and many others like them are false beliefs
so far as the kingdom of heaven is concerned. To win the
kingdom of heaven and to act authoritatively in it requires

that the mind give up its false and limiting beliefs. Two things cannot occupy the same space at the same time. This is true in physics and in metaphysics. That man who finds the treasure in his own subconscious, or spiritual constitution, proceeds immediately to revise all of his attitudes and his opinions. He sells them, in the words of the parable, and with the emotional energy which formerly went into these viewpoints, he buys a treasure of a regnant creative mind.

Any way you look at it, buying and selling is the business of this life. We are all engaged in exchanging the products of our minds and hands. In the external world of commerce and business some exchange the products of the earth, others their manufactured products, and others the products of thought and soul. All our life is one vast system of barter by means of which the singer and the writer, the hardware merchant and the stock broker exchange goods with the farmer and the miner. But we are all merchants in another way. Every human mind is a merchandising business, buying and selling, or exchanging ideas and emotions. So the figure of a pearl merchant always seeking better and better pearls is an apt one. Perhaps from this fact has grown our tendency to speak of special knowledge as "pearls of wisdom." The human mind buys and sells continually. It is always in the market place. If there is any idea on this page which "clicks" with you, then you are in effect saying, "I'll buy that." If you have recently made a mistake, you are in the position now of analyzing the situation and discovering your error; then you must sell the error or dispose of it. Banish it from the stock of your mind forever, and replace it with the truth which the error implies. This is psychological buying and selling with a profit. But in many cases people just buy and sell with no profit.

Take the case of a friend of mine who believes that he catches cold because someone else sneezes in his face. And as he believes, he invariably experiences. All winter long he is buying and selling cold remedies. Nearly everyone he meets, who sees his suffering, offers him a cold remedy, a sure-fire cure. If they describe it well, his enthusiasm rises, and he buys the idea. He tries it and fails. But he will buy another one next day, and be disappointed with it. He is a busy merchant, but he gets nowhere fast. There is no profit to his merchandising. There will be none until that hour when he sells back into the market place all the foolish ideas which he has collected about colds. With the enthusiasm that he has wasted upon all of these, let him buy the truth of the kingdom of heaven, or the pearl of great price. Let him buy insight into the fact of his own psychological independence and the possibility of his own physical freedom from the plaguing colds.

One has to sell his false knowledge in order to have enough psychic money to buy the good knowledge. And the good knowledge is the knowledge of the law of the mind. It is the pearl of great price because it costs all your other and opposing beliefs, opinions and practices. When the rich young ruler came to Jesus (Mark 10) and asked what he should do to inherit eternal life, or continuing happiness, Jesus told him to keep the commandments. This he said he had done all of his life.

> Then Jesus beholding him loved him, and said unto him, One thing thou lackest: go thy way, sell whatsoever thou hast, and give to the poor, and thou shalt have treasure in heaven: and come, take up the cross, and follow me.

> And he was sad at that saying, and went away grieved: for he had great possessions.

> And Jesus looked round about, and saith unto his disciples, How hardly shall they that have riches enter into the kingdom of God.

> Mark 10:21-23

This is the story of us all, but not in the way in which thousands have popularly supposed. The person who is rich in houses and lands and stocks and bonds and money in the bank is not necessarily the rich person spoken of here. A person is not necessarily evil because he is rich, nor good because he is poor. The riches spoken of here are the false beliefs and erroneous opinions of the human mind. The human being is eager for learning from the time he opens his eyes and ears, and every puzzling sight and sound increases his spirit of inquiry. He asks and gets answers, but they are not always the right answers. The road of science which tests the answers, and formulates the right questions to get the right answers, is a long one, and a slow one, and comparatively few travel upon it. The rest eagerly equip themselves with opinions, and beliefs, superstitions, fear, anxieties, and various methods of defense against these. They build up complicated philosophies of opposition against an evil and an error supposed to be without. The mind gets rich in its knowledge of disease, warfare, of failure and of suffering; rich in the knowledge of many things that are not true. Such a rich man cannot enter heaven until he divests himself of his riches. How hardly shall he do that! But many have done it and many are doing it. We own and possess and experience only that which we value most. The pearl of great price is the awareness of one power and one cause in the midst of all phenomena. The perception of this causes the mind to sell all of its other viewpoints, and to buy this one as the supreme learning of the mind.

THE PARABLE OF THE DRAGNET

Again, the kingdom of heaven is like unto a net, that was cast into the sea, and gathered of every kind:

Which, when it was full, they drew to shore, and sat down, and gathered the good into vessels, but cast the bad away.

So shall it be at the end of the world: the angels shall come forth and sever the wicked from among the just,

And shall cast them into the furnace of fire: there shall be wailing and gnashing of teeth.

Matthew 13:47-50

"THE KINGDOM OF HEAVEN is like unto a net that was cast into the sea and gathered of every kind." The human mind is like a net, and we are all fishermen, whether with lines or with nets, fishing either in the sea of our own unconscious depths or in the psychic sea that rolls around us, or both. Our conscious or objective life rests upon our subconscious or subjective life. As a man thinketh in his heart, says Solomon, so is he. Thinking in the heart is essentially subjectivity or feeling. This subjectivity in which your conscious life rests, as a continent rests in the ocean, is full of all sorts of impulses, drives and psychic energy patterns, both good and bad. This is your own personal sea in which you often go fishing.

You have often engaged the mind in reverie or fantasy, for example, and allowed the various pictures and images within the depths of your own mind to swim into your awareness. This is catching fish with your mind as the net. For your awareness is like a net which catches and holds within a certain area of light certain movements of the otherwise dark and unconscious world. But at this subconscious level of life you are one with every other person's subconscious, and some simple experiences in telepathy, which you surely have had, or heard about, will make you realize this fact of oneness. This is the larger sea and in it are moving all the thought-forms and moods of all the people and creatures in the world. It is a vast psychic sea filled with good and bad forms of life. For the thought-forms of the sinner and the saint, the just man and the criminal, are all mixed up in this sea. You are always fishing in this sea whether you choose to do so or not, because your mind is like a net continually being drawn through the sea, and it automatically catches what is in its path, or what swims into its path.

This parable, like the two before it, stresses the need for judgment and discrimination, the selection of what is good and the rejection of what is bad. For in reverie and in fantasy, and even in prayer, the mind can bring in a motley catch. Then it must proceed to select the best and discard the worst. We do well to realize that the best and the worst are in us all, and not to be too much disturbed or chagrined if, after years of constructive thinking and prayer, we still discern certain primitive impulses swimming in our psychic sea, and coming occasionally into the focus of the mind's awareness. Jesus, in the parable, points out clearly what to do when you gather of every kind. Draw the net to shore and sit down and gather the good into vessels, or your established concepts and convictions, but cast the bad away. He who knows the creative authority of his own mind is confident of his own ability to choose and select and to reject. It is as simple as that. What you do not want and categorically deny, will not stay with you. What you love or are interested in, has a home with you, and the greater your love and your interest, the more it will flourish.

This universal psychic sea in which we move is full of the

joys and the griefs, the pleasures and the pain, the fears and
the faiths of millions of people. Depression sweeps over your
mind; you have netted an ugly fish, and a fish unfit for food.
Proceed immediately to do what a deep-sea fisherman off the
coast of Maine, for example, would do if he brought up his
nets or lines and found that he had caught haddocks and
cods, and that gray, sharklike fish which swims in those
waters. He would take the shark fish and beat its head over
the side of the boat, and throw it back as food for the sea gulls
and other fish. But the cod and the haddock he would put in
his basket for his own consumption.

   The good and the bad are always found together in this
world, and good and bad are relative values. "One man's
meat is another man's poison." So each one must know how
to select what is good and reject what is bad. There is one
standard to guide the thinking and the meditation, and therefore the selective function of all mind, and Paul gives it in
these words:

> . . . whatsoever things are true, whatsoever things are hon-
> est, whatsoever things are just, whatsoever things are pure,
> whatsoever things are lovely, whatsoever things are of good
> report; if there be any virtue, and if there be any praise,
> think on these things.
>
> Philippians 4:8

Make every image, thought and impulse pass this test. Make
this your basic, fundamental and over-all master plan, and
it will become the subjective and objective, the subconscious
and conscious standards by which you choose and select
what is proper for your life and reject what is bad. Thus
you will avoid many of those foolish situations which plague
many religious people, the extreme of which is found in
the case of a person who, hearing of prayer and guidance,
and understanding that God speaks to man in the still, small

voice within him, announces that God has guided him to murder his neighbor, or his wife, or husband, or someone. He has heard a voice from within indeed, but all the voices from within are not of God. Merely because they come from that mysterious realm of the subjective does not mean that they are endowed with superhuman wisdom, or with the authority of the angelic host. Far from it. They are often less than human. People who speak in tongues or out of trances are often regarded with awe, and great store is put by what they say as though it were oracular wisdom. Sometimes it is. In many cases it is not. In many cases it is rubbish and nonsense, or simply a repetition of the confused judgments of the conscious mind.

"Test the spirits," says Paul, "to see whether they be of God," and in the preceding quotation he has given us a rule by which to test the spirits and see whether they be of God. If you say I want only what is in divine law and order, or I want divine right action, or I want my true place, you build a rule into the mind which automatically rejects a lot of useless intrusions and prevents many false starts. What is more, when you are confronted with a complicated and confusing situation, this principle of judgment which by your previous meditations you have built into your mind, will come to your aid and enable you consciously to judge quickly and decisively and to select what is right and reject what is wrong.

Conclusion of the Sermon by the Sea

The Parable of the Dragnet is the seventh parable spoken by Jesus in the Sermon by the Sea. The peroration is itself a parable, making eight in all. As the speaker draws to a conclusion he says to his audience: ". . . Have you understood all these things? They say unto him, Yea, Lord. . . . Therefore," he continued, "every scribe which is instructed unto

the kingdom of heaven is like unto a man that is an householder, which bringeth forth out of his treasure things new
and old." (Matthew 13: 51-52) The scribe was a learned
man who wrote out the law. Scribes classified and arranged
the precepts of the law. In the parable, therefore, any person is likened unto the scribe who writes out the law clearly
in his own understanding and delineates it carefully so that
the law of life, or good, and only the law, is his mentor and
his guide in all things.

Such a mind is also like a householder, for such a mind is
now at home in his own house and is keeping its own house.
Before the mind learned good judgment, according to the
law, it was not the keeper of its own house, for wandering
fears and itinerant anxieties often intruded and possessed
the house of the mind. In other cases the mind was given
over to quarrels and arguments with the mere merchandising
of ideas. So that when the master understanding arrives, it
has to go into the house with a scourge of cords and cast out
all those who traffic in merchandise.

If you have considered the parables thus far, and have
allowed them to work upon your mind with their own peculiar and life-changing truths, then it should be neither
amiss nor difficult for you to feel that Christ has been instructing you. If your viewpoint has been changed, then a
whole new world is before you. Yet the good things, certain
aspects of your past life, are not destroyed. This is not the
kind of revolution that destroys all vestiges of the old order,
where the books of the old dispensation are burned by the
fanatics of the new one. The new life and the new man are
not products of destruction, but rather of selection and a
new order of thinking. The same old world, with its forms
and its sights and sounds, remains, but it is rearranged now
for the mind of the new thinker in Christ. It is characteristic of immaturity in any field to set the old too quickly

aside as soon as it has found the new. But spiritual maturity, like all other forms of maturity, recognizes that all that is old is not bad and all that is new is not good. A one-sided lover of the old to the exclusion of the new, yearns for the "good old days," fills his house with crude and ugly antiques, and assumes that all virtue lived in the long-ago. A one-sided lover of the new is sure that none were ever so illumined as he and his contemporaries. He wants everything in modern line and dress. He treads scornfully over the treasures of the past.

Of course, neither is right. The true man sees that truth is everywhere and in every time, and he who has its token may commune with it in any form or dress. He delights in the beautiful and the good because it is beautiful and good in itself apart from any association it may have. And so for such a mind the old platitudes and the ancient verities are refreshingly new and vital, more exciting than the morning news, whilst the latest discoveries of science are but exciting confirmations of the old values. Such a mind is not vexed and troubled by either past or future, but is benefited by them both. It is like a householder in a beautifully furnished home. He has many treasures and objects of art. Some are of value to him and to him alone, because of personal associations. Some have intrinsic value. Some are new and some are old. All are beautiful and all are helpful and useful. That mind which is initiated into the kingdom of its own heaven is not primarily concerned with creeds or opinions or viewpoints or beliefs, but with truth, that is, the constructive current of its own consciousness which rides above all opinions and beliefs. Things that are old and things that are new contribute to this current. Therefore the mature mind makes use of them all.

THE LAWS
OF THE
MIND

2

HOW THE MIND WORKS

THE PARABLE OF THE LABORERS
IN THE VINEYARD

For the kingdom of heaven is like unto a man that is an householder, which went out early in the morning to hire labourers into his vineyard.

And when he had agreed with the labourers for a penny a day, he sent them into his vineyard.

And he went out about the third hour, and saw others standing idle in the marketplace,

And said unto them; Go ye also into the vineyard, and whatsoever is right I will give you. And they went their way.

Again he went out about the sixth and ninth hour, and did likewise.

And about the eleventh hour he went out, and found others standing idle, and saith unto them, Why stand ye here all the day idle?

They say unto him, Because no man hath hired us. He saith unto them, Go ye also into the vineyard; and whatsoever is right, that shall ye receive.

So when even was come, the lord of the vineyard saith unto his steward, Call the labourers, and give them their hire, beginning from the last unto the first.

And when they came that were hired about the eleventh hour, they received every man a penny.

But when the first came, they supposed that they should have received more; and they likewise received every man a penny.

And when they had received it, they murmured against the goodman of the house,

Saying, These last have wrought but one hour, and thou hast made them equal unto us, which have borne the burden and heat of the day.

But he answered one of them, and said, Friend, I do thee no wrong: didst not thou agree with me for a penny?

Take that thine is, and go thy way: I will give unto this last, even as unto thee.

Is it not lawful for me to do what I will with mine own? Is thine eye evil, because I am good?

So the last shall be first, and the first last: for many be called, but few chosen.

Matthew 20:1-16

THE LAWS OF THE MIND are stringent, as the following group of parables will show. People are too accustomed to thinking that happiness and misery are a matter of chance. It's fate, or that's life, they say, and penetrate no further. But man's experience, individually and collectively, is the result of man's consciousness. Consciousness is the sum total of all man's subjective and objective impressions and awarenesses. These in turn are the result of thinking and of dealing with ideas. The individual mind is nothing more than a collection of impressions; some are coordinated and organized into concepts and orderly modes of thinking; many are disorganized and uncontrolled. Mind is a medium for ideas and impressions. Ideas induce emotional flow, or the flow of the spirit, and the spirit is creator and maker.

Notice how good news, when coming to the mind as an impression, starts an emotional flow which animates and exhilarates. It heals and it strengthens. Bad news does just the opposite. It weakens and debilitates. There is a law of the mind which works for weal or woe. When a person understands this law he is able to observe it for his happiness and turn it to good account in his daily living. The Scotch boy, James Watt, noticed that steam escaping from the steam kettle on his mother's stove forced the lid off. This gave him the idea of forcing steam into a cylinder which contained a piston. The expansion of the steam forced the piston back and drove wheels. This was the beginning of the steam engine. Watt's invention was the application of a natural law to higher and more specific ends and purposes. Instead of allowing steam to run wild, he harnessed it and hitched it to the tasks of man. How much labor this little invention has saved man, and how much joy and pleasure it has brought to generations!

In a similar way there is a general law of the mind which can be observed, understood, and then applied to specific ends and purposes to alleviate misery, destroy failure, increase health and happiness, and in general improve a man's lot in life. Now, a law is good or bad according to the way you use it. The law in itself has nothing to do with sentiment, or ethics, or any question of what is good or what is bad. The law is the law and it is always the same, mathematically accurate and just.

The laborers in the vineyard illustrate the law of agreement. Whatever the mind agrees with, it will experience. Nothing is more infallible than this. The thing I feared has come upon me, observed Job. It is not usually the prophets of doom, who shout and rant loudly about the wrath to come, who actually suffer and endure that wrath. It is the less vocal and silent people who are fearful and tense and anxious in their hearts, whose imagery runs to negatives, who experience what Job experienced. It is these people, and there are millions of them, who need to be taught that the opposite is also true, that any positive vision, that any constructive imagery which the mind agrees with, will be brought by the law of mind into the individual experience. This is the good news of the kingdom of heaven, and it is the burden of the teaching of Jesus. But in order to be able to discipline one's mind and make it hold constructive imagery, it is necessary to understand the law just as it is, apart and separate from one's own feelings in relation to the works of the law.

If you are a student of the Bible you know that God made a covenant with Israel. That means that the creative power is in contract with a certain kind of mind called Israel. It implies, too, that the creative power is in contract and covenant relationship with every individual human mind. The essence of that contract is simply this: that whatever any individual human mind beholds, accepts and agrees with, the creative power will honor that acceptance and agreement with the name of action, function and expression. Before this parable is given in the gospel story, Jesus is talking with Peter and the other disciples. He has just told them that it was easier for a camel to go through the eye of a needle than for a rich man to enter heaven. Meaning, as we have previously indicated, not a rich man in the sense of money and stocks and property necessarily, but a rich man in the sense of a mind filled with an accumulation of ideas and impressions and moods, many of which are false. The sense mind which has gathered thousands of sense impressions and has built elaborate theories based upon them, neglecting the spiritual factor, cannot enter into the kingdom of heaven until it divests itself of some of its holdings and buys that one principle, or pearl of great price, which alone can throw a shaft of light and order into all of the perplexing sense impressions.

But Peter is still not too clear about this because he says: "Behold, we have forsaken all and followed thee. What shall we have therefore?" Peter is concerned about what he is going to get. He is judging the whole thing as a *quid pro quo* proposition. He is not apparently satisfied with his own act. He is looking for a reward. Peter's sense of values is still in the outer, external world. At this point he has not sufficiently regenerated to see and accept the values of the kingdom of heaven. Jesus answers him in words that strongly suggest that his reward and every other disciple's reward is simply an ordered and disciplined mind in control of itself. To a sense-bound mind this is no encouragement. It is, rather, disappointing and discouraging. Our incentive in this world is tied to things. The average man is externalized in his outlook and attitude. He looks for outer rewards and punishments. He cannot understand, for instance, that virtue is its own reward because virtue is a state of mind which precipitates external rewards as well as inner peace and strength. He cannot understand that if a person has a strong and stable consciousness of the abundance of good everywhere, that he has all. Therefore the spiritual workman is always endeavoring to achieve such a consciousness. What he does externally is incidental to this. He is somewhat indifferent to the rewards and punishments of the outer world.

But the laborers in the vineyard are typical of those people who live in one world alone and do not know that another controls them. They see everything in outline form only, and they reason only from what is apparent and obvious. They try to square things up by external arrangements, to make things match, and to establish justice. But there is no perfect justice in the external world. There are people lying in prison today who have committed no crimes, but the evidence was against them. They have no friend or newspaper to speak for them, and certainly they have no friend inside them in their realization, and so they must suffer the inhumanity of society. On the other hand, there are criminals of the worst type at loose in the world who will never be apprehended and punished. How do you square this? In only one way: the consciousness of every individual is different. We are all living at different levels. But we are all experiencing the exact results of our own consciousness. The consciousness of freedom commands freedom, and the consciousness of confinement confirms itself in fact and experience. Many good people suffer outrageously because in spite of their goodness they still have a consciousness of misery, and the expectation of reverses. Many a rascal rolls in luxury and enjoys the approval of his fellows because, being void of conscience or remorse, and refusing to condemn himself, he has the kind of consciousness which precludes danger and onslaught from without. Of course, all evil defeats itself and is punished eventually, but the mills of the gods grind slowly, and in such cases the reaction of the law may take longer than one generation.

The reader who has never thought about these things will find that his ideas of justice are challenged and even upset

and confused by this argument. And that was the situation
with the laborers in the vineyard. They were expecting justice of a certain standard kind. But all of a sudden the brands
are changed. The old product is no longer available. And that
is the way with life. For life is the employer of us all. It
comes like a householder into the market place to hire workmen for its vineyard. Some of us are there early in the morning, eager and willing to agree with Life for a penny a day.
So we go to work and we toil all day. Then at the end we
receive the wages we agreed upon. This is justice. Some of
us don't get to the market place until later in the day. We
awaken late to the uses of the mind. But the moment we are
there, Life is there ready to employ us, and Life says: "Go
ye also into the vineyard, and whatsoever is right I will give
you."

Now in the parable, as in life, this happened all day long
up to and including the eleventh hour. All the laborers
agreed with Life. Those who were hired early in the morning made an agreement for an exact amount—a penny a day.
In the morning they thought this was just. In the evening
they thought it was unjust. What changed their mind? It
was greed, and it was envy, and it was anger. And these
ugly emotions were all based upon judgment by circumstances and appearances rather than by the law of the
contract. They compared themselves with others. In the morning when they went to work they expected that at the end
of the day they would receive the penny which had been
agreed upon by them and the employer. But at the end of
the day, when they looked at what the others got, they
changed their expectation. But it was too late to change,
for they had already agreed.

The parable is illustrating the justice of the kingdom of
heaven, the kingdom that is the spiritual side of our life.
In the natural world our ideas of justice are incomplete,

based upon appearances and upon the idea of rewards and punishments. Rewards, in the sense that Peter expected something because he had given up something else. In our natural, everyday life, we naturally expect that a man who works overtime shall get overtime pay, and that one who works little shall earn little. This is fine as far as it goes, but when we try to apply it as an over-all rule to our lives, it breaks down because it does not take into account the factor of the individual consciousness. The parable is conveying the teaching that there is an higher order of justice than that which is based upon appearances and external arrangement. That higher order of justice is based upon the law of agreement. What you agree with you will get. What you accept in consciousness you will receive in experience. Jesus points out elsewhere: ". . . If two of you shall agree . . . as touching anything that they shall ask, it shall be done for them of my Father which is in heaven." (Matthew 18:19). This is a simple statement of the law that whatever the conscious and the subconscious minds agree upon the spirit will validate and create. If you agree on a penny you will receive a penny, no matter how much effort you put into it. All around us are the effortful ones striving and struggling to attain, but always attaining only what they have accepted in consciousness. Around us, too, are the effortless ones whose work contains a minimum of struggling and striving and they, too, attain, not according to the measure of their struggle and effort, but according to their consciousness of acceptance. This is justice in the kingdom of heaven, and it scatters our old ideas of justice as we learn them on the earth. We cannot change our thinking until we change our ideas, or until we get new ideas. If you get a new idea out of this parable, the idea will modify your thinking and change it. Then you will enter into a new heaven or state of consciousness and that will automatically make you a new earth or manifestation of consciousness. "Behold I make new heavens and new earths."

PARABLE OF THE TALENTS

For the kingdom of heaven is as a man travelling into a far country, who called his own servants, and delivered unto them his goods.

And unto one he gave five talents, to another two, and to another one; to every man according to his several ability; and straightway took his journey.

Then he that had received the five talents went and traded with the same, and made them other five talents.

And likewise he that had received two, he also gained other two.

But he that had received one went and digged in the earth, and hid his lord's money.

After a long time the lord of those servants cometh, and reckoneth with them.

And so he that had received five talents came and brought other five talents, saying, Lord, thou deliveredst unto me five talents: behold, I have gained beside them five talents more.

His lord said unto him, Well done, thou good and faithful servant: thou hast been faithful over a few things, I will make thee ruler over many things: enter thou into the joy of thy lord.

He also that had received two talents came and said, Lord, thou deliveredst unto me two talents: behold, I have gained two other talents beside them.

His lord said unto him, Well done, good and faithful servant; thou has been faithful over a few things, I will make thee ruler over many things: enter thou into the joy of thy lord.

Then he which had received the one talent came and said, Lord, I knew thee that thou art an hard man, reaping where thou hast not sown, and gathering where thou hast not strawed:

And I was afraid, and went and hid thy talent in the earth: lo, there thou hast that is thine.

His lord answered and said unto him, Thou wicked and slothful servant, thou knewest that I reap where I sowed not, and gather where I have not strawed:

Thou oughtest therefore to have put my money to the exchangers, and then at my coming I should have received mine own with usury.

Take therefore the talent from him, and give it unto him which hath ten talents.

For unto every one that hath shall be given, and he shall have abundance: but from him that hath not shall be taken away even that which he hath.

And cast ye the unprofitable servant into outer darkness: there shall be weeping and gnashing of teeth.

Matthew 25:14-30

Parallel passage in Luke 19:11-27.

THIS, ALSO, is a parable about justice and about the law as it is in the kingdom of heaven. Use is the lesson here. Use determines all qualities, whether good or bad. Don't use what you have and it will rust away. Use it, and you increase it, whether it is a muscle, an idea, or a tool, or money. In this parable also the elements of adventure and risk and daring are implied. Don't be overcautious. Strike a bold blow for freedom and advancement. Better go down fighting for what is right than rot suffering what is wrong. All this is apparent in the parable at the ordinary level of understanding.

But the parallel and higher meaning of this parable increases our understanding of the science of thought and the way of the spirit. The parable is speaking about money and how money is used. The talent was not a coin but a certain weight of silver, of money in the raw, so to speak. Money in the raw is gold or silver or precious jewels or, in the case of the American Indian, wampum, which is exchanged as a symbol of value. In the days of the California or Yukon gold rush, a miner came down out of the hills with a bag of gold dust. He went to the Government assayist's office and put the bag of gold dust on the counter. The man behind the counter put it upon a scale and balanced it with certain weights, and then gave the miner currency of the day. Sometimes gold dust wasn't exchanged for currency. The gold itself was currency. A certain weight of gold dust was gladly accepted in exchange for groceries or clothing or implements of business.

It is in somewhat this sense that the talent is spoken of here. It is a certain measure or weight of silver. And in the parallel meaning of the parable it means a certain measure of life, or psychic energy. For we all come with certain endowments differing in measure and degree. Some of us have a strong psychic tide running, some have only small swells. Some people have a strong sense of capacity and power to be and to do and to have. They have strong desires and drives which send them forward industriously and courageously. Millions of others, on the other hand, are more hesitant, doubtful, and more awed by circumstances and facts. They are not endowed with a boundless energy, and in facing the obstacles and challenges of life they tire and retreat easily. But many of those less highly endowed can be taught to realize the deeper strength and talents which are native to their beings but which are not in evidence or in function at first. And this proves that the gold is in every person. It is not always on the surface in the beginning of a person's life, but it is there, and it can be drawn out and realized at any time. Our literature is full of instances of people who started with great handicaps and small talents, but by industry and zeal they dug out the precious stuff within themselves and purchased life and achievement with it. An immigrant boy pushes a fruit cart around the streets of the city, but he saves his money and invests wisely and in time becomes the world's greatest banker. This is an actual American story. In one way or another it has been duplicated thousands of times.

There is no mystery in the matter of increasing one's wealth by wise investment in this world. The ways and means are evident on every hand, and a little study and application will enable anyone to have success in this regard. But to handle the real money or silver and gold of life is another matter. But it is the burden of the parable. Jesus says that a man investing his money wisely in this world and doubling it is like the kingdom of heaven. We must discern what this likeness is. The money of the kingdom of heaven is simply consciousness or awareness. Some of us are more aware of life's meanings than others. The more we are aware the more we can do. But everybody can increase his awareness. How many educated, knowledgeful people cannot make money because they have the consciousness of limitation! How many capable people earn good money but it slips through their fingers because they have the consciousness of limitation! There are brilliant and capable men from all walks of life on the Bowery. They lack the consciousness that coordinates their knowledge and capacity with action and accomplishment. People say that their disease is alcoholism, but that is only secondarily so. Their primary disease is spiritual. They are out of touch with their God-self where the gold lies. They are down on themselves emotionally. Drinking is only the symptom of the real trouble. They are well equipped, not only to earn a good living but to rise high in life, because many of these men have already been there. But looking down on themselves they have no consciousness of self-acceptance and expansion. Their thoughts buy nothing but misery and self-abuse.

On the other hand, there are all around us people not heavily endowed with brains, skills or education, who make money hand over fist. They have the Midas touch. Everything they handle turns to wealth. With them nothing succeeds like success. What is the difference in those several groups of people? Consciousness, and only consciousness. Mind is the only buying power in this world. Believe greatly and you can buy greatly. Believe little, and you won't have the money to buy even a living. Mind, then, is currency. More particularly and precisely, it is the currency of the kingdom of heaven. It is psychic stuff. It buys all things including health and happiness.

In view of this, what is meant then by the parable of the talents? We have seen that a parable has two parallel truths. One is fairly obvious and in this instance it is the fact that a man went on a journey and left some money with three servants, five talents of silver to one, two talents to another, and one to a third. What is the parallel of this? It is the action of the spiritual money, or the currency of consciousness. These three servants represent ourselves at different states or levels. We are all like the five talent man because we all have five senses. This is the mind with only sense knowledge or learning. Some philosophies maintain that all

of our knowledge comes through the five senses. Were this
true we would be without hope. For when the senses cease
to report good sights and sounds and other sensations of
encouragement, then the consciousness of confidence and
courage would fail. This is exactly what happens to the
average sense-bound mind. It judges by appearances and
when appearances fail, it is cast down. But the spiritual
thinker knows that there are five other senses, the spiritual
counterparts of the ordinary five, making ten in all. These
inner or spiritual senses report spiritual facts which transcend the material world.

For instance, there are two kinds of sight. One is the
ordinary sight by which we perceive objects through the
reflection of light from the objects to the retina of our eyes.
The other kind of sight is the sight of understanding by
which we perceive ideas and meanings. When someone
explains a situation and you say, "Oh, I see!" that indicates
inward sight. The five inner senses lay hold of an inner
world of significance and reality. All maturity leads to the
development of the inner senses and perception. That is
why the kingdom of heaven is like a man who was given
five talents and doubled his money. The five senses
cannot exist alone. They do not lay hold on truth. They
need the spiritual senses to complement them. The spiritual senses are developed somewhat in every individual,
but the degree of development is the thing that determines
the significance and the happiness of an individual life. The
physical senses report the facts of the physical world and
they are often discouraging. Unless a person has a healthy
development of the inner senses which report the world of
spiritual truths and thus bring courage and strength above
and beyond the ordinary senses, then that person is in distress and conflict, for his desires impel, and the physical
facts of life repel. The ideal man is one who has the inside

and the outside world well balanced. His inner sense of spiritual reality is great enough to modify and even to transcend any discouraging circumstances in the physical world. This is what is meant by the five-talent man doubling his money in the kingdom of heaven. It is a doubling of perception. It is an increasing of faith and the consciousness of the goodness of life. The ordinary five-sense mind is limited by its surroundings. It takes the cue for its thinking from what it sees. Its moods are generated by the moods of the race. But the mind of spiritual sense ranges outside, above and beyond its environment, and sees and hears what the outer senses cannot know. All effective prayer or constructive thinking is correcting what you see and hear by what you know. Circumstances suggest defeat, but the spiritual thinker remembers that circumstances are not causative, that mind is causative, and so establishes hope and faith not upon an external view of things, but upon an internal knowing. He thus sustains a constructive consciousness and this is money in any realm. It is negotiable. It has purchasing power in any market.

The two-talent man represents something similar, but lower down in the scale of the consciousness that commands. The five-talent man has had to discipline and train his ordinary five senses in order to win the five inner senses. He has had to work in and upon himself. The two-talent man doesn't know much about discipline, but he has strong drives and impulses toward good. He has a vigorous desire to grow and to expand and to create and to achieve. He is zealous and industrious. This kind of mind knows little or nothing about the laws of the mind, but it accomplishes by its great native drive and vigor of action. This kind of person is not a philosopher necessarily. He does not necessarily think much about anything but what is immediately before him. He is objective and extroverted. For him there are only two things to consider: himself and the world immediately in front of him. He has confidence and "push" and is not easily thwarted. Such a mind doubles its money. It increases its capacity and its consciousness of its own ability.

The one-talent man is a vegetable. He has no strong instincts or drives. He hesitates, doubts and waits. Instead of acting upon his world he allows the world to act upon him. He is afraid even to desire better things because it may be "against God's will." He is overawed by events and by the apparent sovereignty of facts. He recognizes only the outside world. He feels no inner reality, no inner drive and push to modify the outer world. Yet he is endowed with the greatest force and capacity there is. Because he is a man, a mind, he has been given the one talent, the capacity to think. The law is in him but he knows it not. He has buried it, and it lies dormant and inactive. This mind is centrifugal, revolving around its own center. It never dares to fly off and establish a new orbit of life. Such a person's line of force is bent back into and upon himself. Basically there is no difference at all between this man and the man who had five talents given to him and who doubled his money and therefore had ten. In numbers, ten is simply the one with a zero beside it to show that the one has been active. The one-talent man has the one great treasure of life, but he does not recognize it. It is buried in the earth of himself, that is, within and beneath his materialistic consciousness and sense-bound mind. Such a person is doomed to repeat his present experience endlessly. He cannot change. He has accepted a doctrine or a creed of life which forbids change. He has buried enterprise within his negative and defeatist opinions. He is the kind of person who says: You can't do that, or there is no cure for this, or it has never been done that way before. It is silly to him to suggest that with God all things are possible. In a great many cases this kind of man will watch his loved ones suffer and die in fulfillment of his belief that there is no hope, rather than to try anything new. In fact, he opposes the new. He fights change.

A person cannot change unless he changes his ideas. But to change one's ideas one must get a new viewpoint and a new standard of judgment. Otherwise one's ideas will simply be a repetition of the old in different dress. The new standard of judgment which will produce new ideas is the understanding of the law of the mind. But this is buried in the one-talent man. It must be dug out of oneself and put to use. This, then, is the parallel meaning of the parable which lies right alongside the obvious meaning that a man who has a piece of money or ability and doesn't use it, loses it. Anything unused withers away. Not only that, but it changes to its opposite. And thus in the parable the Lord took away the one talent and gave it to the man who had ten. Nothing succeeds like success and nothing fails like failure. Use your consciousness of the presence of God in the rough and tumble of the world or you will lose it. There is no peace save to the strong. The one-talent man with his practice of ignoring or not using his own power of thought will soon forget that he has any. Initiative in industry will be taken away. Confidence and faith will leave him. But they will go and accrue to the account of the man who "stepped out on God and his law." Whatever one's consciousness is, it is always being magnified and extended within and without. If you have a consciousness of unfailing supply and increase, it will magnify and grow. But if you do not know the higher law, or do not set it in motion daily by your definite, directed thinking you will think in terms of limitation and limitation, when it is "magnified," is merely more limitation.

In the higher level of the parable's meaning, the three men in the parable represent three kinds of consciousness,

and therefore three different measures of life. The three
men represent three different measures of awareness, which
is the coin and the currency of the kingdom of heaven.
Every state of mind, good or bad, is a kind of awareness,
stamped with the invisible image of the king of the universe. It has authority and purchasing power. It is legal
tender for every transaction in human experience. It is the
coin of life. It is current everywhere at every time. It purchases life.

THE PARABLE OF THE TEN VIRGINS

Then shall the kingdom of heaven be likened unto ten virgins, which took their lamps, and went forth to meet
the bridegroom.

And five of them were wise, and five were foolish.

They that were foolish took their lamps, and took
no oil with them:

But the wise took oil in their vessels with their
lamps.

While the bridegroom tarried, they all slumbered
and slept.

And at midnight there was a cry made, Behold,
the bridegroom cometh: go ye out to meet him.

Then all those virgins arose, and trimmed their
lamps.

And the foolish said unto the wise, Give us of
your oil; for our lamps are gone out.

But the wise answered, saying, Not so; lest there
be not enough for us and you: but go ye rather to
them that sell, and buy for yourselves.

And while they went to buy, the bridegroom came;
and they that were ready went in with him to the
marriage: and the door was shut.

Afterward came also the other virgins, saying,
Lord, Lord, open to us.

But he answered and said, Verily I say unto you,
I know you not.

Watch therefore, for ye know neither the day nor
the hour wherein the Son of man cometh.

Matthew 25:1-13

AFTER DISCUSSING the Parable of the Talents, we can follow
the meaning in the story of the ten virgins easily. Our senses
are called virgins because they are feminine. They are feminine because they are impressionable. They are receivers.
Sight and hearing, taste and touch, and smelling, are movements of mind which receive impressions from our surroundings. Our personal and individual mind is nothing more nor
less than the sum of its impressions. Thus it is important
what impressions the mind is made of. In the Biblical view,
each of us is a person of ten senses, and like the ten virgins
we go forth to meet the bridegroom, or ideal of life, to whom
we seek to be joined. We seek to meet, to marry and to be
indissolubly united with the highest and the best kind of
understanding and experience. But half of us is foolish and
half of us is wise, and we, therefore, meet not the ideal but a
mixture of good and bad. This is the common experience.

In the parable the right use of the mind is suggested by
the five wise virgins. The five outer senses are the foolish
ones because they receive only the impressions of the material world. They gather impressions of danger, failure, disease, hurt and old age, and suffering. They report happy
things on occasion also, but their reports are usually a mixture of good and evil. All expectation of good based upon

sense knowledge is predicated upon the turn of events and changes in the material world. Thus it is limited, partial, and subject to a wide margin of error. Every one of us is always looking for his ideal or for the bridegroom, but since the sense knowledge is not adequate, we are like the five foolish maids without enough oil in their lamps. The oil was for light, and light means the perception and clarity of the mind. In the material world you cannot find a continuing line of prospects to cheer and sustain the mind in faith. You cannot find your ideal in the material world alone. The sense world contains no oil to sustain the light of the mind.

The mind needs its inner perceptions of truth in order to see its way to the ideal or the good life. And that is why the mind of the kingdom is likened to five wise virgins who are well stocked with oil. They have light. They can see. They make their way easily to the house where the bridegroom is. The mind which knows the creative power of thought and the corresponding impotence of materiality has oil to sustain its hope and its progress until it arrives at its goal.

This parable is the purest example in mental science. No one meditating upon it from this standpoint can fail to find his own powers of creation and accomplishment enhanced. Our minds are impressed through the senses. Whatever impresses us leaves its seed with us. The seed grows up into function and action. When we allow the outer world to impress us with fear, anxiety, envy, greed, or sloth, then by the automatic action of the mind we give birth to the unlovely brood these will father. But the mind itself is ever virgin, inviolable and unspoiled by its impressions. As was said in ancient Egypt so still it can be said of the human mind: "I am Isis, goddess of ten thousand appellations. No man hath ever me unveiled." The human mind was destined to unite with one and only one, her true lord, the truth, or the good. Whatever your mind conceives of as good is your lord and bridegroom, and you are on the way to union with your conception of yourself. You want to be impressed by goodness and beauty and truth, by harmony and achievement and satisfaction. All these compositely and ideally are the bridegroom of the mind. Only the inner senses can find the way. Let them lead you. They have inner evidence of his presence. As you follow them you withdraw attention from the outer and so the outer senses go to sleep.

For example, suppose you are looking for health. The consciousness of health is the bridegroom you seek. You wish your senses to be impressed by this consciousness of health. If you look at the suffering body and describe its symptoms you will not be impressed by health but with quite the contrary. Therefore, in a scientific prayer for health we are taught to withdraw the attention from the thing that we do not want and put it upon the thing that we do want. In this case the thing we want is health. So first of all we would vision health, and then we would fill in the picture and teach the mind the reason for health and impress it with the conviction of health. We would remember that disease is not something independent of man. It is a condition of man. Since all conditions are in the last analysis states of mind, and mind can be changed, then the present condition is subject to change. The supreme law is the law of consciousness and thought. Knowing this, we rise above the fear of something which has us in its power, and we immediately have it in our power. This impresses the mind with hope and confidence. We continue such a line of reasoning until the mind is impressed by assurances which increase in strength until the mind is at peace and happy in its union with the conviction of health and well-being. It has found its bridegroom and is married to him.

You will see that in such a meditation of the mind there

is a weaning away of the attention from one set of impressions to another. The light lessens on one side and increases on the other. In the parable the five foolish virgins cannot see because they have no oil in their lamps. The parallel meaning here is that when the mind is filled with directed attention and disciplined meditation, we, like the wise virgins, pass from fear to faith. The outer senses cannot see the reason for fear any more. They are dulled and stilled. The world is no longer threatening. The light of faith is strengthening and the light of facts waning in the mind's experience. The conviction that the mind's ideal is present and is more sovereign than the mind's previous experience is deepening and gaining strength. The mind is passing from conscious anxiety to subconscious faith. The lights of this world are going out. The lights of an inner world are coming on as they do every evening when the sun, or the light of this world, sinks, and the heavenly bodies, or the lights of the heavenly world, appear. The inner senses, or five wise virgins, are united with that which they sought, the mind's purpose and its goal. The door is closed, and those sense impressions which were toward fear, trouble and distress, cannot enter in. This is the mind that knows faith.

THE PARABLE OF THE WEDDING ROBE

And Jesus answered and spake unto them again by parables, and said,

The kingdom of heaven is like unto a certain king, which made a marriage for his son,

And sent forth his servants to call them that were bidden to the wedding: and they would not come.

Again, he sent forth other servants, saying, Tell

them which are bidden, Behold, I have prepared my dinner: my oxen and my fatlings are killed, and all things are ready: come unto the marriage.

But they made light of it, and went their ways, one to his farm, another to his merchandise:

And the remnant took his servants, and entreated them spitefully, and slew them.

But when the king heard thereof, he was wroth: and he sent forth his armies, and destroyed those murderers, and burned up their city.

Then saith he to his servants, The wedding is ready, but they which were bidden were not worthy.

Go ye therefore into the highways, and as many as ye shall find, bid to the marriage.

So those servants went out into the highways, and gathered together all as many as they found, both bad and good: and the wedding was furnished with guests.

And when the king came in to see the guests, he saw there a man which had not on a wedding garment:

And he saith unto him, Friend, how camest thou in hither not having a wedding garment? And he was speechless.

Then said the king to the servants, Bind him hand and foot, and take him away, and cast him into outer darkness: there shall be weeping and gnashing of teeth.

For many are called, but few are chosen.

Matthew 22:1-14

Parallel passage in Luke 14:16-24

THE KINGDOM OF HEAVEN is like a wedding feast. It certainly is. A great supper is spread where all may eat bread in the kingdom of heaven. The food for the hungry mind is available. The answer to every problem is here. Strength for the weary, hope for the failure, confidence and peace of mind for the distressed and storm-tossed, are laid out in lavish abundance. Let all who are bidden come to the feast. All human beings are bidden to this feast, and all human beings will some day sit down to table in the kingdom of heaven to eat the food which the great King of Life has provided for them. And the occasion is not mere mealtime but a wedding. A wedding such as we have described in the last parable where the mind is united with its true desire.

This parable not only presents a fine figure of the individual human mind and the way it works, but also of the mind of man in general. The great feast is spread, but those who are bidden do not come. The truths of life are here. For thousands of years they have been taught. The principles and laws by means of which mankind could live in health and harmony and happiness have been made available. But mankind spurns them, makes excuses and turns his back upon them, and busies himself with every perversion. Those who ought to be at the table consuming the spiritual truths are not there. The philosophy and religion and science of the world are too busy with externals to heed the call to the wedding feast. This parable is addressed to the Pharisees, those meticulous observers of all the minute details of the Levitical law with regard to ceremonies, tithes, and purification and so forth. The Pharisee then and now is one who believes in an external form of righteousness, who congratulates himself on the merits he has attained through some external acts of obedience. He justifies himself, as Nicoll says, "by outward acts and behavior."

Heaven is within a man and a man must move within himself in order to realize heaven. That is, he must change and work over his ideas and opinions and concepts. But the

Pharisee lays stress on the outer side of things, and because he is bound by external meaning and by the literal things of the senses, he cannot move internally in himself. He puts no value upon internal movement, and therefore Jesus said of him: ". . . Ye shut the kingdom of heaven against men: for ye enter not in yourselves, neither suffer ye them that are entering to go in." (Matthew 23:13) The Pharisee is found not only in religion but in philosophy and in the sciences, also. Obsessed by literal and external meaning, he either omits entirely or makes light of the internal side of life. Physical science, for example, is too much concerned with fighting disease rather than discovering the source of disease. This is the social state of man, but it is also the individual state. The mind becomes lost in external concerns and forgets the one thing that could solve its problem.

From that moment when in our crib the eyes begin to focus and the ears begin to locate sound, and all the other senses begin to function, we are primarily aware of the world around us, the world of things and forms and shapes and sound. As time goes on, we may become dimly aware of a world within. But real awareness of the inside world and of its tremendous significance in our daily lives comes only when we rise to that level of consciousness which is called the kingdom of heaven. Man becomes absorbed in the forms and shapes, and in the movements of things. Educated in the ways and in the processes of matter and its laws, he generally makes light of the ways and the laws of the spirit. It is usually after much suffering or reverses of some kind that the ordinary man gets truly interested in the spiritual side of life. Many who have been religious all of their lives have never gone to the great feast. For the wedding feast does not imply the practice of an external form of religion. The great king sits on his throne within every individual and spreads a feast fit for the gods. He asks only the attention, the consideration, and the interest of your mind about certain great truths of life. He asks this not in the manner of a schoolteacher, bending your mind to study, but in the manner of a gracious host offering you the supreme delights of the table.

The kingdom of heaven is not onerous. It requires change, and change is hard and often painful. But once changed, a person finds the delights of the kingdom more than worth it. At the king's table you may eat of strength and of confidence and peace of mind, and drink long drafts of inward satisfaction. And are not these, after all, the things that matter most? Are these not translatable everywhere in the world into health and wealth and goodwill, and all the satisfactions of the outer life? They are indeed, but the average mind schooled in matter does not realize it.

Those who are bidden to the feast do not always come, and those faculties of our own mind which should be at the feast tend to turn away. This feast is a wedding banquet at which your mind with its chief desire, goal or purpose, is to be married to the matching mood or the proper emotional support from within. At the wedding feast the mind will be feeding upon the knowledge that there is one power; that the things it formerly feared are therefore no longer tenable; that that one power is thought power, and therefore it, the mind, is endowed with the power to create its own conditions. As the tensions and the fears fall away and are replaced by confidence, and faith, and good cheer, then the mind is married to what it formerly hoped for, and the hoped for thing takes on the name of action and function.

Scientific prayer is not a prayer of petition in which the mind begs an unknown God for favors. But scientific prayer is rather a wedding feast at which all the assembled faculties and attitudes of the mind gather with great joy and rejoice and laugh and sing in the presence of the great king.

But there is one guest without a wedding garment in the parable story. Our minds wear spiritual·garments just as our bodies wear material clothes. The mind itself is invisible, but we know it through what it does. It sees, it hears, it tastes, it touches, it smells through our senses. It thinks and it reasons; it rejoices and it is sad. The way in which it looks or hears or thinks or feels is its garment. Its many attitudes are the garments which it wears. The mind must have its proper garment to fit the occasion, just as in external, bodily life we do not wear sports clothes to a wedding, or a bathing suit at dinner. A wedding guest at the banquet of the great king in the kingdom of heaven should have on the proper garment, or he doesn't belong there. When you pray you assemble all of the faculties and attitudes of your mind for the purpose of being wedded to something which is at present outside of yourself. It is something that is desirable. It is the beloved, and the desired, but it is not yet one with you either in realization or in function. Prayer is a whole-souled action. There must be no mental reservations, no unfinished business, in the mind. There must be no unredeemed emotions, such as resentment or ill will, or quarrelsomeness. These are wedding guests without garments. They are present but they don't belong. Pretense, subterfuge, insincerity, words without feeling, hope without faith, any one of these may sometimes creep into the prayer process of the best of persons. When you find him at your wedding feast deal vigorously, quickly and ruthlessly with him. For the kingdom of heaven is like the man in this story. He said: "Bind him hand and foot . . . and cast him out into outer darkness." That is, immobilize him immediately. Prevent him from handling anything with his hands at the banquet hall, and prevent his feet from moving, and throw him into the forgetfulness of mind.

All of your attitudes are assembled at the wedding feast

when you pray for union with something higher than your
present self. It is not merely your attitudes toward the beloved that are involved, but it is your attitudes, for example,
toward all other people. You cannot isolate the parts of the
mind, and you cannot leave your prejudices and resentments
behind you. Not only your religious views and opinions are
involved in the prayer process of the mind, but all of your
other attitudes and viewpoints. For example, your political
and economical and social viewpoints—these are gathered
wherever your mind is concentrated. They may be in the
background, to be sure, but they are there. They are guests
at every operation of the mind. If any of these viewpoints
of yours cause you distress or agitation or unrest when you
think of them, then they are not proper guests at a wedding
banquet of the mind. Any attitude or sense of guilt or self-
condemnation or remorse is in the same category. If they are
present in your mind when you assemble the mind for
prayer, they are wedding guests but without garments. For
these are atttitudes of dissention, separation, loss, weakness
and failure. Certain parts of the mind are wearing these
attitudes as garments and do not belong at the feast. For
every attitude at a wedding feast is concerned with union
and joy. The whole mind must move concertedly in one
direction, and that is toward complete and joyful union with
some higher form of good. When you fail to demonstrate
the law of faith in your daily life, look for a wedding guest
without a garment.

3

RENEWING THE MIND

THE PARABLE OF
THE CLOTH AND THE WINESKINS

Neither do men put new wine into old bottles: else the
bottles break, and the wine runneth out, and the bottles perish: but they put new wine into new bottles,
and both are preserved.

Matthew 9:17

Parallel passages: Mark 2:22, Luke 5:36-39.

JESUS CHRIST solved men's problems. He healed bodies and
minds. He used a science. If anybody solves any kind of
problems he reveals that there is a wisdom that existed before the problem. Wisdom is the knowledge of the spiritual
law, and the application of it is a science. The preceding
group of parables indicated the nature of the law in cold,
clear, bare and unsentimental outline. The present grouping
of parables suggests what the mind should do with its under-

standing of the law, for unless we act, it is as though we did
not understand. Having seen the law in all of its bold
clarity, we must next respond and act with courage and
daring.

The Parable of the Cloth and the Wineskins

There is nothing harder for us in this life than the acceptance
of a new idea. The best evidence of this is the fact that the
world continues to repeat its errors. Human beings go
around and around in the old routine, rather bearing
those ills they have than fly to others they know not of. Fearful of change, they rarely change voluntarily. And because
they will not change voluntarily for the better, life forces a
change upon them for the worse. Isaiah and Jesus paint the
picture very clearly, as we find it in Matthew 13:14-15:

> And in them is fulfilled the prophecy of Isaiah, which sayeth,
> By hearing ye shall hear, and shall not understand; and see-
> ing ye shall see, and shall not perceive:
> For this people's heart is waxed gross, and their ears are
> dull of hearing, and their eyes they have closed; lest at any
> time they should see with their eyes, and hear with their ears,
> and should understand with their heart, and should be con-
> verted, and I should heal them.

It could not be said any plainer. Healing follows upon a
change in the individual, and that means healing in the sense
of making whole, not only the body but the mind in relation
to the circumstances of the individual. But if the eyes can't
see something new, and if the ears cannot hear anything new,
and if the heart cannot feel toward something new, then
there can be no conversation or turning around, and the love
of God, which would otherwise heal us, is impotent. The
kingdom of heaven is a spiritual-mental realm, and therefore
the whole basis of life in that realm is thoughts and moods.

They are the basis of life outside the kingdom of heaven, also. Therefore, if one would change, one's thoughts must change as well as one's feelings. One must have new ideas, for feeling is the result of ideas and one cannot feel in a different way if he retains his old ideas. It is our concepts which produce our moods. Emotional distress is directly traceable to opinions and concepts which offend or disturb the mind and thus awaken disturbing emotions. God says that he made a good world and he approves of it. (Genesis 1:31) But man is inclined to disagree, and his disagreement costs him his peace and pleasure in this world. The human mind knows too many things that aren't good, too many things that it is afraid of, unduly concerned about. It spends days and nights in anxiety about external conditions to which it attributes the power of causation. It is at the mercy of its beliefs.

Now Jesus teaches that you must change your belief if you want to experience a different world. He teaches that the kingdom of God is here. The world that God made is here, and it is altogether lovely and beautiful if you can see it. But if your eyes are dull, the good world does not exist for you. Yet the teaching of the parables is designed to fall upon your mind and awaken your senses to their higher possibilities, so that you may see the good world all about you, peopled with good people; and hear the sounds, and feel the emotions of peace and confidence, of love and goodwill. It is not only altogether possible, it is a reality now, for many people are living in such a world. You can live there, too, if you follow the Master in one simple operation of the mind: get a new mind, by changing your ideas. And that's what is meant by putting new wine into new wineskins.

Wine represents the quickening element of the spirit. Wine or liquor is the one element in the external world which most nearly represents the new spirit which a man has in the kingdom of heaven. For wine, like raised bread, is the product of the mysterious. process of fermentation. The first miracle which the Christed man performs is the turning of plain water into wine, and every individual who sees and understands the law and acts upon it, setting it into operation in his life to change his mode of living, will most certainly follow in the footsteps of the Master, by changing the plain water of his life into that spirited and exhilarating element called wine.

Grant the creative power of your own thought and you have, with one fell swoop, cut the ground from beneath all fears and anxieties, resentments and hates, and have, at the same time, established a basis for confidence and goodwill. Carry this forward, and your whole emotional life will change. You will feel buoyant and happy, confident and free. The vexations and hurts of the past will be swallowed up in forgetfulness. You have the wine of life, and it causes you to forget the bad and to experience the good. But you can readily see why you cannot put and hold this new wine of life in the old bottles, or the old concepts and viewpoints of the mind. If you hold to the old viewpoint that things and people and conditions and situations are responsible for your success or failure, your health or happiness, your good or ill, then you cannot, on this basis, sustain the moods of confidence, goodwill and joy. These viewpoints cannot hold the wine of life.

The parables were written in a day and in a land where wine bottles were made from the stomachs of sheep. A wine bottle made from a freshly killed animal was soft and pliable, and capable of great expansion, and therefore when it was filled with new wine it allowed for fermentation and expanded with the fermentation of the wine. An old wineskin had lost its moisture and its oils. It was no longer resilient. It would not stretch. So an old wineskin was safe only for old wine which had finished its fermentation. The analogy is well-nigh perfect, as most of Jesus' parables are. If you wish to grow, you must live with growing things.

The other part of the parable repeats the lesson in another way. A patch of new cloth upon an old and threadbare garment lasts only for a short time until the old garment gives way at the edges of the patch. The old cloth is weak and cannot hold the new and stronger piece. You may have a beautiful picture of the brave, new world you want to inhabit, but you will need a new philosophy in order to live in that brave new world. You may have fine ideas, but you will need to think in a new way in order to carry them out. You may hold the ideal of the Fatherhood of God and the Brotherhood of Men, but if you have prejudice toward any person or toward any group, your ideal will remain an unreal thing. You cannot put the strong cloth of brotherhood upon the old attitude of prejudice. If you yearn for confidence and poise but at the same time believe in the power of people and situations to make you fearful and anxious, you will always be nervous.

In the Greek myths, Procustes was an odd host. We shudder when we read of his hospitality. He bade every traveler try his bed, and if the traveler was too long, Procustes cut off his legs, and if the traveler was too short, Procustes stretched his legs to fit. But perhaps there is a good side to the myth. Every aim and goal and purpose in life calls us to make ourselves to its measure. A slothful man cannot be successful in business. Business demands that he be busy. The teacher cannot prize money above wisdom. The scientist in his laboratory finds in the mysteries of nature his greatest reward, and the mysteries fascinate him and bend him to their service. The metaphysician cannot merely hold thoughts, and hope that thoughts will make him health, or money, or fame. But he must give himself to the thoughts

and allow them to hold and to mold him into their own likeness. Jesus must not become the prisoner of the church, but
the Christian must become the prisoner of Jesus, and be fashioned according to his mind and will. The human mind
must learn to relax, to give up, to open and release the old
before it can receive the new.

THE PARABLE OF
THE WICKED HUSBANDMEN

Hear another parable: There was a certain householder,
which planted a vineyard, and hedged it round about,
and digged a winepress in it, and built a tower, and
let it out to husbandmen, and went into a far
country:

And when the time of the fruit drew near, he sent
his servants to the husbandmen, that they might receive the fruits of it.

And the husbandman took his servants, and beat
one, and killed another, and stoned another.

Again, he sent other servants more than the first:
and they did unto them likewise.

But last of all he sent unto them his son, saying,
They will reverence my son.

But when the husbandmen saw the son, they said
among themselves, This is the heir; come, let us kill
him, and let us seize on his inheritance.

And they caught him, and cast him out of the vineyard, and slew him.

When the lord therefore of the vineyard cometh,
what will he do unto those husbandmen?

They say unto him, He will miserably destroy

those wicked men, and will let out his vineyard unto other husbandmen, which shall render him the fruits in their seasons.

Jesus saith unto them, Did ye never read in the scriptures, The stone which the builders rejected, the same is become the head of the corner: this is the Lord's doing, and it is marvellous in our eyes?

Therefore say I unto you, The kingdom of God shall be taken from you, and given to a nation bringing forth the fruits therof.

And whosoever shall fall on this stone shall be broken; but on whomsoever it shall fall, it will grind him to powder.

And when the chief priests and Pharisees had heard his parables, they perceived that he spake of them.

Matthew 21:33-45

Parallel passages: Mark 12:1-12, Luke 20:9-18.

As we have seen thus far, the parables are stories about everyday life which have parallels in the mental, psychological and spiritual life of man. The mind is like a vineyard. It is a cultivated area of consciousness. In the universal or unconditioned consciousness, every individual lays out his own working area and cultivates it with his thoughts and attitudes. On or in this area of personal consciousness, each one raises his own bread and wine and nourishes his life. After the flood, Noah, whose name means rest, laid out a vineyard and began to be an husbandman. This is the first instance in the Bible we have of this analogy, and it follows all the way through to the end. As was indicated earlier, from the moment we open our eyes as babies, we are eager for knowledge. The hungry senses devour the world around us. We want answers to every question and reasons for

every sound and sight. The child is notorious for his repeated use of the question "Why?" When we cease to in-
quire, we cease to grow.

But we must have some answers to our inquiries, whether
those answers be true or false. And with these answers we
hedge our vineyard about. No man can know everything, but
every man can know something. The limits of each individual's knowledge are like the hedge about a vineyard.
The dominant viewpoints and general attitude are the
boundaries of the mind. These boundaries represent the
places where the mind is satisfied with its own opinions and
refuses to entertain anything more. Every mind has some
philosophy. It has its beliefs about politics, religion, about
health and happiness, and a future life. If its beliefs satisfy
it, or if it finds it difficult to go beyond a certain vague impression and can reason no further, the mind stops there and
that is like the hedge about the vineyard. The chemist operates within a certain defined area, the lawyer in a different
area. Each and every one of us has his homestead or his plot
of ground in the vast consciousness of God. Each has his
winepress, or the workings of his own mind, which give to
him his measure of zest and hope and courage, and each has
his tower, or his philosophy of strength and endurance, by
means of which he guards his mind against the enemies of
gloom and defeat. Every person has his attitudes and outlook and emotional pattern, and these are like the husbandmen which work the vineyard. According to the cast of a
man's mind, so shall his reward be. Or, as Solomon says, as
a man thinketh in his heart, so is he. The mind has its tenants and workmen just as the literal vineyard has. And when
the tenants do not produce, the wise man replaces them
with more industrious ones. Every man has a right to expect
results from his thinking, but if he continues to keep false

opinions and limiting and negative beliefs as the tenants of his mind, these will kill all hope and expectation that he sends to receive his fruits. All those ideas and opinions which tenant the average human mind, and which do not owe allegiance to the creative sovereignty of the spirit in man, are sources of weakness. The spirit is the Lord, but these false tenants kill the Lord's emissaries until in many cases they capture the mind itself and cast it out of its own vineyard, as in neurosis, or kill it, as in insanity.

There is one thing, and one thing only, which keeps the mind healthy, and that is the knowledge of the presence of God and its daily practice.

THE PARABLE OF
THE REJECTED CORNERSTONE

Jesus saith unto them, Did ye never read in the scriptures, The stone which the builders rejected, the same is become the head of the corner: this is the Lord's doing, and it is marvellous in our eyes?

Therefore say I unto you, The Kingdom of God shall be taken from you, and given to a nation bringing forth the fruits thereof.

And whosoever shall fall on this stone shall be broken: but on whomsoever it shall fall, it will grind him to powder.

Matthew 21:42-44

EUCLID'S FAMOUS forty-seventh proposition says that the square of the hypotenuse of a right-angle triangle is equal to the sum of the squares of the other two sides. If you have ever watched a builder lay out the foundation of a new building you may have observed him making use of this mathematical principle in geometry in order to square the corners of the foundation. The corner determines the angle of the walls. If the corner is square the walls will be square. Shape a stone in accordance with the forty-seventh proposition and set it level as a corner, and it will automatically determine all the other angles of the building.

So it is with Christ, who is figured by the simile of the rejected cornerstone. Christ is the head of the corner. There is no building or structure of any stability without that wisdom called Christ. If you have a United States dollar bill handy, turn it over and look at that part of the great seal of the United States which bears a pyramid. You will notice that the pyramid is in two parts to represent the material and the immaterial aspects of life. The immaterial or spiritual life is represented by the capstone which is suspended above the pyramid. This capstone is not a stone at all, but an eye, or a point of light. Among many significant things, it means this: that the cornerstone or capstone of our life is awareness, light or understanding. The pyramid represents man, and man can be considered from two points of view. From a physical and evolutionary point of view man is a biological being, with his roots in matter, and he ascends by aspiration and development to a heavenly or a spiritual element above him. Considered from the opposite point of view, each person is a point of light or consciousness which generates with perfect accuracy a four-square reproduction of itself in matter. All of this is a symbolic way of representing the great truth that thought is creative, and that all phenomena stem from this as the walls of a building start from a cornerstone.

This truth is a stone, concrete, hard and impervious. There is no human logic or experience which can refute it or de-

stroy it. You cannot break it in pieces no matter how you try. But it is a rock of offense and a stone of stumbling to millions who refuse to be responsible for their own acts, who cannot bear to accept the fact that the causes of their misery are within themselves, who want something to save them without any action or change on their part. That mind which is schooled in the philosophy of mechanical and chemical causes, finds it utterly illogical to postulate consciousness as the supreme truth of our existence. In this sense there are many atheistic Christians in the world in spite of their stout affirmations of belief in the spiritual power. Everywhere and at every hand the world of men stumbles on this stone and is broken in confusing, suffering pieces. We try to heal sick bodies by every possible means except by the force and wisdom which generated the body in the beginning and can alone repair it. We say we believe in God, but if at the same time we believe in powers which can destroy God's handiwork, then our avowed devotion to God is not quite whole and sincere. God is a jealous God and wants your whole-souled conviction, not merely your mental assent.*
A man who in the business world would never think of welching on a contract may inadvertently and unwittingly do so with his God, or with the spiritual law. Then when his prayers are not answered, he ascribes the decision to a God outside of himself. He says that God didn't want him to have what he prayed for. But God is law as well as person, and he acts by his law. If he gives you the desire or the promise, he also gives you the fulfillment, and the method for fulfillment. If there is any error between desire and fulfillment, that error is in the human mind and its beliefs rather than in God.

These are only a few of the ways in which we stumble

* See Ten Words That Will Change Your Life, p. 50.

on the cornerstone of life. Many millions of people do not
stumble upon the stone, necessarily, they merely ignore it as
long as they can. Being endowed with natural strength and
optimism, they succeed by nature and are healthy and happy.
They find no need to reason beyond the material fact of
their life, or beyond the ritualistic forms of religion. I know
a man who was born wealthy and who has doubled his
wealth in a long and very successful life. He is a good man,
as men go, but he has no spiritual understanding. The spiritual world and its laws are vague and meaningless to him.
Everything he ever turned his hand to has succeeded. He is
a power in his community. He is respected and admired.
Everything he ever wanted he has achieved, until now.
There is one thing he wants which he cannot get: the love
of a particular person. His personality and the state of his
consciousness preclude it. Habits of thinking and emotional
patterns which were insignificant at one time, and went un-
noticed, now have become formidable bonds and ugly movements in the consciousness. Because he does not know the
principle of thought he cannot change his thought, and hence
he cannot change himself. He is bound by the reactions of
his own thinking, but does not know it.

Hence it is said that of some they stumble upon the stone
and are broken to pieces, but on others the stone falls and
grinds them to powder. No one can with perfect safety
ignore the spiritual facts of his being and the daily need of
prayer. The human mind is susceptible to influences all
around it, both good and bad. Daily prayer separates these
influences and casts out the bad, and thus no unfortunate
reaction is allowed to build up. But one who ignores the
spiritual constitution of his being and goes blithely on his
way, forgetting to correct his thought, picks up a good many
negative influences unknowingly. In many cases failure of
health or business will halt a man in his wayward progress

and cause him to stop and think and go back to basic spiritual causes. When this happens, the stone has fallen. If a person will not apprise himself of the stone, the stone will apprise the person of itself, grind him to powder, because it destroys and obliterates the man's own philosophy and all of his old way of living. A person who has been brought to his knees with all of his ego and pride beaten out of him, knows that there is something in life which is stronger than he. When he sees it he becomes a new man, and the old man is ground to powder.

Thus this great truth of the supremacy and primacy of consciousness is a formidable fact and is therefore called a stone. Men build machines which can grind any rock upon the earth into sand and powder. But here is a spiritual rock which grinds men to powder, and cannot itself be broken. "Behold, I lay in Zion for a foundation a stone, a tried stone, a precious corner stone, a sure foundation: he that believeth shall not make haste." (Isaiah 28:16)

THE PARABLE OF
THE WISE AND FOOLISH BUILDERS

Therefore whosoever heareth these sayings of mine, and doeth them, I will liken him unto a wise man, which built his house upon a rock:

And the rain descended, and the floods came, and the winds blew, and beat upon that house; and it fell not: for it was founded upon a rock.

And every one that heareth these sayings of mine, and doeth them not, shall be likened unto a foolish man, which built his house upon the sand:

And the rain descended, and the floods came, and
the winds blew, and beat upon that house; and it
fell: and great was the fall of it.

Matthew 7:24-27

Parallel passage: Luke 6:46-49.

THIS PARABLE is not difficult when taken close upon the heels
of the Parable of the Rejected Cornerstone. The analogy of
a good foundation is understood by nearly everyone. But it
is easy to miss the spiritual import, nevertheless, of this
parable. As we learned in the Parable of the Sower, it is possible to hear and not hear, so that the facts of consciousness
and mind and thought and faith may be heard by the outer
ear but not penetrate to the understanding.

Every person dwells in the house of his own consciousness
built out of his thoughts and moods, attitudes and reactions.
For some it is a house of peace and shelter, refreshment and
rest. For others it is a place of torment, full of worries and
fears, guilts and quarrels. God told Solomon to build him a
house where he would dwell, a sanctuary for the presence of
God, and this is the proper use of every person's mind, to be
a sanctuary for the presence of God. In that presence is
fullness of joy, composed of thoughts of peace and harmony,
of confidence, assurance, joy and goodwill. But when Jesus
came to the temple of his day, he found it not a sanctuary
for the holy presence but a den of thieves. And taken sym-
bolically, it refers to the human mind which more often than
not is a den of thieves, a collection of worries and tensions
and vexations which keeps the mind in continual unrest and
disturbance. But "Except the Lord build the house, they
labour in vain that build it." (Psalm 127)

The foolish mind builds its house of faith out of externals
and when these shift and change in the storms of life, his
house of faith goes down also. When a man's philosophy of

success is built upon confidence in his own brain and other human powers, his success is bound to fall when the storm comes, as come it will. For the brain and all human powers fail at times, and only the spirit remains. But if a man has built up his house of consciousness without taking his spirit as his major premise, then it has no fundamental strength, and some wind will topple it.

The wise builder, then, builds his house of consciousness upon that same rock which was the cornerstone of our spiritual-material habitation here. We have seen that that rock is impervious and unbreakable. It breaks others and grinds them to powder, but nothing can break it. A philosophy of life and a mode of living that is built upon that, as its major truth, is proof against all of the storms of life.

THE PARABLE OF
THE UNFINISHED TOWER AND THE
KING'S RASH WARFARE

And there went great multitudes with him: and he turned, and said unto them,

If any man come to me, and hate not his father, and mother, and wife, and children, and brethren, and sisters, yea, and his own life also, he cannot be my disciple.

And whosoever doth not bear his cross, and come after me, cannot be my disciple.

For which of you, intending to build a tower, sitteth not down first, and counteth the cost, whether he have sufficient to finish it?

Lest haply, after he hath laid the foundation, and

is not able to finish it, all that behold it begin to mock him,

Saying, This man began to build, and was not able to finish.

Or what king, going to make war against another king, sitteth not down first, and consulteth whether he be able with ten thousand to meet him that cometh against him with twenty thousand?

Or else, while the other is yet a great way off, he sendeth an ambassage, and desireth conditions of peace.

So likewise, whosoever he be of you that forsaketh not all that he hath, he cannot be my disciple.

Luke 14:25-33

IN THE Parable of the Hidden Treasure, we saw what it means to give up the lesser for the greater, though that lesser include at the present time the totality of our possessions. In business life we often have to liquidate in order to get enough cash to buy another worthy property, which is more profitable in the end. And we have to do the same thing with our psychology, not once, but over and over again. The Christ is the great light in the Scriptures. He represents the best and the highest of man. And every man should seek for that best and that highest, not outside, but within himself. "Christ in you," says Paul, "the hope of glory." And Isaiah prophesies that the holy child which shall be born and which shall be a saviour of his people, shall be called Emmanuel, which means God with us. The sense of God's presence built upon a philosophy of inward causations and responsibility is the great good we are all after, for it will provide for us all other forms of good, such as health and happiness, success and harmony.

But one has to understand enough of what that good is in

order to be attracted to it, and in order, therefore, to lay down all that denies it. So Jesus says that one, in going toward that goal, has to turn his back upon his own father and mother, upon wife and children, and brethren and sisters, yea and his life also, otherwise "he cannot be my disciple." This business of turning against your own family must not be taken literally. No case can be made for it. There is nothing in any real religion which requires you to hate your own family, or even a stranger, for that matter. Moses uses a similarly strong statement when he encourages every man to take his sword and slay his neighbor. What is meant by all of this? Remembering that the Bible is a story of spiritual men, we must not get bound up in the idiosyncrasies of literalism. It is true that the child must one day turn his back upon parents and family and go out and live his own life, but this is not hating in the literal sense. But a person must learn to hate, literally, such things as prejudice, and anxiety, fear and depression of spirit; in short, all of the errors of human thinking and feeling. He must learn to despise these as unworthy of the spiritual stature he wants to achieve. He must be ruthless with them and put them to the sword, to the death. And only when you are as determined as this with the terrors of your own mind, will you rout them out and cleanse your house so that the Holy One may come and dwell therein.

Furthermore, Jesus points out that you must learn to bear your own cross and "come after me." How greatly have Christians throughout the ages missed the positive and triumphal side of Jesus' teaching! They have thought of the cross only as a symbol of suffering. True, they have spoken of the triumph of the cross, but the words have had a hollow sound, for there appears to be no triumph. Christianity has too often emphasized the way of the cross as "feet cut by jagged stones, and shoulders raw from the chaffing of a cross," but Jesus endured the cross "for the joy that was set before him." (Hebrews 12:2) Cannot we find out what that joy was? And is it also set before each one of us? And if so, is it big enough and grand enough to attract us above all else, so that we shall let go of lesser values and lesser loyalties? To take up the cross means not only to take up suffering and pain, it means to take up a new idea which promises good, to embark upon a new course of mental and emotional action which will end in good. But as we indicated in the Parable of the Wineskins, this is the hardest thing for man's mind to do—to take up a new idea. He tends to cling to the old. Like the prisoner of Chillon in Byron's poem, he has been so long in prison that he has come to love it. His natural love of freedom has been so long unexercised that it has withered away. But if a man would have freedom he must desire freedom, and he must dare to work for it. There must be a change inside, and this is hard. It involves pain.

There is pain in the way of the cross. There is pain in breaking away from the old and advancing on something new. But it is a birth pain. For if it is endured courageously, it subsides in rejoicing over the new. People think that they are carrying a cross just because they are suffering. But they are only suffering and to no good end, and for no real purpose. To carry the cross may indeed involve suffering, but it has its end, its purpose and its goal, right here on earth, within this span of life. People's value sense is most often tied up with the money of this world. If a thing costs a great deal of money, they think it must be worth more. If it is sold too cheap, they value it less. A certain self-service store, for example, had been selling a certain jar of food for fifteen cents, but it wasn't moving. The manager of the store, who was a good merchant, had the price changed and the article was thereafter advertised at two for thirty-one cents, and it sold like hot cakes. Housewives thought they were getting a bargain. It is the exceptional person who can distinguish value apart from price. But it is a faculty every one of us must learn to develop, especially as related to the values of the kingdom of heaven. For that which may be held by the world in great estimation is useless and valueless in the kingdom of heaven. And the values of the kingdom of heaven the ordinary world mind cannot appreciate. It counts them as insignificant and, like the swine, would trample pearls in the mire. For the wisdom of this world is foolishness with God and therefore " . . . If any man among you seemeth to be wise in this world, let him become a fool, that he may be wise." (I Corinthians 3:18)

Man's whole advance into the kingdom of heaven is by means of determining relative values. In fact any kind of advance on any scale, on any level, requires choice between two values. If something means more to you than another thing, you will choose that and follow it. If it seems important to you to get control of your own mind and your own emotions and thereby control the rest of your world, you will lay aside many of your other activities and proceed in the first endeavor. But as with the wedding guests at the great king's feast, the human mind can find so many excuses for not doing what it ought to do. That is because the value of its true goal has not struck it as being of supreme importance. It is a practical consideration for you to ask yourself if you are willing to give up your old resentments in order to enjoy better health. And again it is practical to determine if you are willing to let go of your human pride in order to have success. Are you willing to be as nothing so that the spirit may be all? It is really not a difficult thing to do when you remember that the spirit can bring you all that you ever desired, and much more besides, if you will take yourself out of the way and allow the spirit to have its perfect will with you. It is practical, too, to remember *not to*

strive after ideals which are at present beyond your consciousness to attain. The promises of God are universal and
all-inclusive. They include any possible good that any human being could desire. But they are realizable by any one
human being on the basis of his understanding of the law
and his consciousness of acceptance. But to desire something which you do not have the consciousness to accept is
the worst kind of frustration and misery. Remember that
with God all things are possible, but not so with Henry
Smith, but Henry Smith may know God and constantly increase his own possibilities and capacities over and above
his former experiences.

Consider then, if you wish to build a tower, have you the
consciousness for it? Can you endure not seeing that which
is invisible as yet? And continually strengthen yourself in
the confidence that it is real? Else you may find yourself in
the position of announcing a grand ideal, yet in your action,
in your living, coming short of it. Many people have stepped
out on faith and won great victories. But it is practical for
every one to determine whether or not he has that faith
before he steps out. Or if, like the great king, you go to en-
counter another in war, it is practical for you to sit down and
consider your relative strength. If you had an ailment in the
body and you firmly declared that you believed that God
could heal it, therefore you resolved to make use of no other
therapy, you would succeed or fail according to your consciousness of God's presence. It is dangerous to have an
idealistic kind of faith, or a faith which is only really a longing after faith, but no actual faith at all. One must learn to
distinguish here. If, while you are relying on prayer alone,
you still believe in physical causation, you may find yourself
in trouble. That is why Jesus lays it on the line and points
out plainly that life in the kingdom is an all or nothing propo-

sition. The mind must gradually give up its beliefs in external causation, its beliefs that things outside of itself can either harm or help it. "My help cometh from thee, which made heaven and earth." Some daily thought and prayer given to these propositions will gradually bring the mind to this wholehearted commitment.

THE PARABLE OF THE RICH YOUNG FOOL

And one of the company said unto him, Master, speak to my brother, that he divide the inheritance with me.

And he said unto him, Man, who made me a judge or a divider over you?

And he said unto them, Take heed, and beware of covetousness: for a man's life consisteth not in the abundance of the things which he possesseth.

And he spake a parable unto them, saying, The ground of a certain rich man brought forth plentifully:

And he thought within himself, saying, What shall I do, because I have no room where to bestow my fruits?

And he said, This will I do: I will pull down my barns, and build greater; and there will I bestow all my fruits and my goods.

And I will say to my soul, Soul, thou hast much goods laid up for many years; take thine ease, eat, drink, and be merry.

But God said unto him, Thou fool, this night thy soul shall be required of thee: then whose shall those things be, which thou hast provided?

> So is he that layeth up treasure for himself, and is
> not rich toward God.   .
>
> Luke 12:13-21

THIS PARABLE is easily understood from our previous discussions of the other parables. A point or two only need be emphasized here. Greed is one of the seven deadly sins according to the ancient thinkers. And greed is self-stealing. Excessive desire is really an affirmation of lack, and since what a man gets and achieves in this life is directly proportionate to his own consciousness, excessive desire or greed will take away a lot more than it brings to him. "Take heed, and beware of covetousness." Bobby Burns' observation of life in general applies especially to the rich fool in this parable: "The best laid schemes o' mice an' men Gang aft a-glay." He planned wisely, shrewdly and brilliantly, but it all went for nothing, because greed ate up his soul, and ruined him.

Again, it may be observed with the Psalmist that they labor in vain who try to build any structure without taking into consideration the building power that is inherent in the mind itself. When you desire anything, know that the desire is God-given and that he who gave the desire will give the embodiment or the expression of it. The next step, therefore, is quietly to accept the desire on no other basis than this, plus the fact that you know that acceptance in the mind is guarantee of manifestation in the outer. This gives rest and nourishment to the mind, and prevents excessive wanting or desiring from eating up its substance. The rich fool in the parable allowed desire to eat up the substance of his mind and, when that was gone, all was gone. All of the parables in this grouping have indicated to us how a person must renew his thinking if he would change his life and his world.

SETTING THE LAW
IN ACTION

4

THE LAW OF USE

THE PARABLE OF THE TWO SONS

But what think ye? A certain man had two sons; and he came to the first, and said, Son, go work to day in my vineyard.

He answered and said, I will not: but afterward he repented, and went.

And he came to the second, and said likewise. And he answered and said, I go, sir: and went not.

Whether of them twain did the will of his father? They say unto him, The first. Jesus saith unto them, Verily I say unto you, That the publicans and the harlots go into the kingdom of God before you.

For John came unto you in the way of righteousness, and ye believed him not: but the publicans and the harlots believed him: and ye, when ye had seen it, repented not afterward, that ye might believe him.

Matthew 21:28-32

THE LAST GROUPING of parables showed us what kind of new thinking the mind must engage in if it would renew itself and thereby renew the body and all external affairs. They not only emphasized the need of new thinking and illustrated it, but furnished and showed the substance of that new thinking by stating and restating the law of mind in motion and its consequent extension in fact and experience. The rest of the parables continue these themes, as did the ones before them, but introduce others also, and in the present grouping we shall see that use and action are emphasized.

The Parable of the Two Sons

The distinguishing characteristic of the teaching of Jesus that sets it apart and above even much of religion that is carried on in his name, is the fact that he does not tell people what to do, but rather what and how to be. He does not make rules for people. He teaches them how to live from within themselves. The whole teaching of Jesus is geared with inner transformation. It has little or nothing to do with external duties and external forms of righteousness. Jesus shows you what to do inside of yourself, with your thinking and your feeling, in order to attain residence in the kingdom of heaven. If one is really in the kingdom, he is changing psychologically all of the time. It is not enough merely to say "I believe," and to give mental assent. The teaching of Jesus is not a code, but a way of life. It is not enough for a man to say that he accepts Jesus as his saviour, unless he can show that Jesus is alive in his changed consciousness.

So it is action that is emphasized in this parable and in many of the others, but especially in the present grouping. A man had two sons and he asked each of them to go and work in his vineyard. One said, "I will," but did not. The other said, "I will not," but afterward he went. This much of the story alone shows very plainly the distinction between words and deeds, and between intentions and actions. We must be careful to remember what the vineyard is, that it is a man's own mind and that that is the place where one ought to be at work. Life is always calling us to go to work in that vineyard, especially when we desire something different in our experience, or when we have been disappointed or hurt by some experience. Then the Father bids us go within and change our own psychology and work with our own thoughts and induce a different spirit. And it makes no difference what we have said or have not said, have believed or not believed; if we do the work in consciousness, we shall receive the reward without. Lay out your vineyard, plant your project, "imagineer" your goal, change your consciousness.

Every problem defines its own answer. If you are hungry, you want food. If you are thirsty, you want drink. If your purse is flat, you want money. If your life is lonely, you want companionship. Don't try to fix your life up on the outside. Make a change on the inside. Go to work in my vineyard. Work with the ideas of solution, as the problems define them for you. Accept the solution and integrate it into your consciousness with confidence, and you shall by no means lack the embodiment or the manifestation of it in your circumstances.

The two sons illustrate the two classes of people in the world. One says I will go, and does not. This is like that type of person who gets very interested in the philosophy of the kingdom but neglects to put it into practice within himself. He has all the words but never the tune. He is exemplified by that typical church-goer found in all religious bodies who says to the preacher on the way out, after the sermon, "That was a fine sermon. Everything you said applies to somebody I know." We can sympathize with him because there is something of him in every one of us. But we must

rouse ourselves from his spell, and get to work in the vineyard.

The other son is typical of those people who make no
outward show of religion, who talk little about their beliefs,
who hardly ever use the phrases and gestures of religion, but
somehow work its essence into their lives. Very often they
are people who have gone off the deep end in error or misery. They have seen the sordid side of life and it drives them
with a mighty reaction in the opposite direction to search
for what is good. They do not need to pose. They have no
false pride left. They have been so far down that their ego
has been well humbled, and so they make great demands
upon life to yield them its real truth and strength, and life
answers them, and that is why the publicans and the harlots
in the Bible's account go into the kingdom of heaven ahead
of those who make a show and a philosophy of religion but
have little practice. The publicans and the harlots, says
Jesus, believed John when he told them to repent. They understood his message that repentance means self-change,
thinking again. But the Pharisee, who justified himself by
outward acts and behavior, felt no need of change. He accepted himself. And so does the present-day Pharisee. And
self-acceptance keeps one at his present level of development
and does not allow him to work and move inwardly. This is
the mind that is typified by the one son in the parable who
said: I will go, but he did not. He was perfectly sincere,
undoubtedly. He wanted to go, he desired to go and he
intended to go. But he did not know that he could not go
because he had accepted himself where he was. And for
these reasons, Jesus says in the Sermon on the Mount, "Except your righteousness shall exceed the righteousness of the
Scribes and Pharisees, ye shall in no wise enter into the
kingdom of heaven."

Let the reader not forget that the Scribes and the Pharisees are perennial and appear in every generation.

THE PARABLE OF THE BARREN FIG TREE

There were present at that season some that told him of the Galilæans, whose blood Pilate had mingled with their sacrifices.

And Jesus answering said unto them, Suppose ye that these Galilæans were sinners above all the Galilæans, because they suffered such things?

I tell you, Nay: but, except ye repent, ye shall all likewise perish.

Or those eighteen, upon whom the tower in Siloam fell, and slew them, think ye that they were sinners above all men that dwelt in Jerusalem?

I tell you, Nay: but, except ye repent, ye shall all likewise perish.

He spake also this parable; A certain man had a fig tree planted in his vineyard; and he came and sought fruit thereon, and found none.

Then said he unto the dresser of his vineyard, Behold, these three years I come seeking fruit on this fig tree, and find none: cut it down; why cumbereth it the ground?

And he answering said unto him, Lord, let it alone this year also, till I shall dig about it, and dung it:

And if it bear fruit, well: and if not, then after that thou shalt cut it down.

Luke 13:1-9

THE PRIMITIVE MIND lives in a world of rewards and punishments. He believes in an unknown God which deals out rewards for good acts, and punishments for bad ones. Jesus scotched this system at every turn. He taught a science of being, which placed rewards and punishments within the thought and act of the individual. He taught the law of action and reaction on the mental plane, and put all the factors within the control of the individual mind. "With what measure ye mete, it shall be measured to you again." He taught as did Hillel before him, that the Golden Rule contains all of the law. "All else," said Hillel, "is commentary thereon."

In other words, as you act toward others both in thought and physical motion, so you shall be acted toward and upon. Today we know this as a fundamental mental law. We recognize more clearly than ever before that "thoughts are things," as Prentice Mulford said; that every thought is incipient action; that every state of consciousness is a prophecy of an experience: that will power is simply the accumulation of repeated thought in a definite direction until it becomes habitual. What goes into the mind as an impression sooner or later comes out in the experience. But sometimes impressions are made in the mind when the person is unaware of it. As we saw in the Parable of the Tares, a man may sow good seed in his field, but when he is asleep or unaware, the enemy, or the negative aspects of one's environment, may sow tares in his field. This is a very important point for the student of the science of things mental and spiritual to remember.

The mind is a receptive medium. The mind never sleeps. It is always awake, even when we are asleep. And so it is always capable of receiving impressions. It receives many bad impressions along with the good ones. Unless by the conscious, deliberate, definite action of scientific prayer we correct the bad impressions which fall upon the mind, they will take root and at some unforeseen time will be precipitated into action and experience. Those who do not know the law of their mind, and therefore do not take precaution to pray scientifically and to correct many of the negative impressions, have what they call "accidents," or they may call the experience fate. They suppose that it was what they call "chance" which brought loss to them instead of gain, or hurt instead of pleasure. But accidents, fate and chance are all words which describe the individual mind's ignorance of the cause behind phenomena and experience.

No man experiences anything but that which comes through his mind or consciousness. But that doesn't mean a man is bad if he has an accident, or a severe illness, or a reversal in his affairs. It may mean that he was careless and failed to take precaution. It is not merely wrong doing according to the accepted code that produces misfortune for us, but inaction and not doing are equally productive of trouble. The mind is always creating, whether for good or for ill. It is never still. But if we do not manage our own minds, they will be managed by the atmospheres and forces around us. If we do not feed our own minds constructive ideas, then the suggestions and intimations from our environment may feed our minds negative ideas. By the creative law of the mind these come to fruit as well as the affirmative ones.

All this Jesus points out in a word or two when he answers the question of some people who told him of the Galilæans whose blood Pilate had mingled with their sacrifices. He said that the Galilæans were not sinners above all the Galilæans because they had suffered these things. They were not bad people because they had suffered misfortune, and all the other Galilæans were not good because they had escaped. Jesus indicates that all are vulnerable whether good or bad, according to the conventions of the day. "Except ye repent, ye shall all likewise perish." In other words, everybody has to change his thinking. Nothing remains static, not even the mind. If you do not consciously and definitely fill it with pleasant things, it will in the natural course of events become filled with rubbish. To make this point clear Jesus told the parable of the fig tree. If the fig tree doesn't produce good fruit, destruction will overtake it. This is the way of evolution and progress. Progress is made by an increase of consciousness. The great drama of evolution from the single cell to modern man portrays and represents this. Our path is out of the darkness into the light.

To increase our awareness and to take more conscious, concerted control of our life is the compelling necessity of race and individual. The primitive organism is the victim of its environment, more or less. It floats about in the water and is carried by the current. It has no means of self-action or self-propulsion. Such a creature portrays a kind of consciousness which is also in man. Man comprehends not only all of the creatures below him, but all of the possibilities above him. But an individual must not allow his mind to indulge in the primitive kind of consciousness. Man is a thinker and he must think in order to move and make progress. Thinking is his means of propulsion. If he stops thinking or thinks only in the sense of repeating old ideas, then he puts himself in a primitive state of consciousness in which he allows his environment to do his thinking for him. He then becomes a victim of the tides and the winds of the race mind. The fears and the anxieties of the race working through his own mind can force the individual into unproductiveness and even destruction. Life demands fruit both of man and of the fig tree. And the fruit which life demands of man is consciousness of his own divine nature. Life demands that the individual becomes aware of his own inherent God-given capacities and powers which enable him to move, to select and to travel in the paths of peace and the ways of pleasantness, and to escape accident, trouble and misery.

But many people are like the fig tree in the parable. They put on a show of life, but they produce nothing. In other words, they are animate, they work and play and move about in life, but they still keep a primitive type of consciousness which fears the unknown, peoples the darkness with demons, and attributes causation to everything but the self. Such people are spiritually dead though physically alive. They do not change their ideas. They move around the same old circles. There is no fruit in the sense of their becoming increasingly aware of higher meanings, capacities and purposes of life. It is no accident that Jesus chose the fig tree rather than the olive, which is just as common in the East, as the analogy in this parable. For thousands of years the fig has been a symbol of spiritual growth and productiveness. The fig bears no blossoms outwardly. It blossoms inwardly. Split open a fresh fig and you will see its myriads of flowers. It was, therefore, always thought of by the ancients as a fitting symbol of the soul of man which bears an inward blossom in the form of awareness and consciousness. What a person does or says or accomplishes externally is the direct result of what a person is inwardly, therefore, spiritually speaking, the real fruit of the soul and the mind is consciousness and character.

But there is always hope for the unproductive one, for the man as well as the tree. Hence, in the parable the vine-dresser begs for the life of the fig tree, saying to the lord of the vineyard: "Let it alone this year also, till I shall dig about it, and dung it: And if it bear fruit, well; and if not, then after that thou shalt cut it down." If the fig tree is healthy in stem and branch and leaf, as is suggested in the parable, then doubtless it is lacking only the right kind of fertilizer to bring out the fruit. Modern agricultural *science* now recognizes that all of the mineral elements necessary to produce fruit may be in a certain soil but "locked up" as they say. The soil is in a stable state and has quit working, so to speak. Good soil may appear inert but is never so. It is an active, dynamic mass of chemical and bacterial movement. Digging about the tree, as the vinedresser suggested, will bring buried minerals to the surface and give the roots freedom and air to breathe. Dunging, or adding organic matter, will provide bacterial action, added nourishment. Of course the Biblical vinedresser did not know all of the scientific reasons for his practice, but he did know what to do in order to get fruit. Dean Sieling, dean of the College of Agriculture and Horticulture, and director of the Massachusetts Agricultural Experimentation, tells of his own experiments which show that the decomposition of bacteria in the soil forms many compounds such as citrates and tartrates. These compounds then act upon the soil particles and release the phosphates which are an important factor in the production of crops.*

Thus there is something that can be done about a live and healthy fig tree which is producing no fruit. There is something that can be done to cause it to produce fruit. The vinedresser and the soil scientist know this. There is also something that can be done about a person whose life is not producing fruit. The spiritual scientist knows this. Life grows out of the universal life. Our roots are in the universal soil. All of the elements that are necessary to productiveness and fruitfulness are there, but they may be locked up and unavailable, until another factor is introduced. That factor is the understanding of the law of mental and spiritual causation. Grant the creative power of your thought, and you have started a chain reaction in the soil of the soul which will cause your enterprises and purposes to flourish,

* In *What's New in Crops and Soils*, October, 1953.

and all of your true goals and objectives to emerge and be realized.

So let us not write off an unproductive fig tree or a spiritually barren man. The most hopeless condition is curable. With God all things are possible. With the knowledge of our own creative power let us dig and dung about our projects and see if they will not bring forth fruit. Then in good time most surely we shall know the meaning of the words: "And he shall be like a tree planted by the rivers of water, that bringeth forth his fruit in his season; his leaf also shall not wither, and whatsoever he doeth shall prosper." (Psalm 1:3)

THE PARABLE OF
THE CHILDREN AT PLAY

But whereunto shall I liken this generation? It is like unto children sitting in the markets, and calling unto their fellows,

And saying, We have piped unto you, and ye have not danced; we have mourned unto you, and ye have not lamented.

For John came neither eating nor drinking, and they say, He hath a devil.

The Son of man came eating and drinking, and they say, Behold a man gluttonous, and a winebibber, a friend of publicans and sinners. But wisdom is justified of her children.

Matthew 11:16-19

Parallel passage: Luke 7:31-35

CHILDREN LOVE TO PARODY the acts of their elders. What grown people do as a serious occupation, children treat as a play. The world of childhood is a world of make-believe and creative imagination. For the child the world is anything he wants it to be. He never lets the crude world of facts interfere with the ideal world of wish and fancy. An old packing crate in the back yard becomes a columned mansion for little Mary when she wants to play house, and some stones from the walk will be sufficient for dishes, with which she will serve tea to her imaginary guests. And little Billy in the living room on a rainy day is not so alone and bereft as the conditions would suggest. Sitting all alone on the living-room sofa he can, by the magic of his own mind, suddenly make that living room alive with Indians and wild-riding cowboys of which he, himself, is the head. Or the coffee table suddenly becomes a wild plain, and any handy object, whether book, or ash tray, or pencil or paper will be a wagon or a hill or a train or a whole army. Out on the street or in the playroom the little Billies and Susies and Marys may get together and play at weddings and funerals, and at all of the other things that seem so important and serious to grownups. One little fellow ran into the house one sunny morning and called to his mother, "Mother, we found a dead cat and we are going to have a funeral!" In a very short time he was back announcing that they didn't hold the funeral because the cat was "too dead." There is nothing troublesome or formidable to a child in its play. That which to the adult seems like an abrupt and erratic change, is to the child a perfectly smooth and natural transition of interest. And nothing is ugly or hurtful to the child when he is "in play." There is nothing wrong, and everything is right, in the world of play and make-believe.

As Max Eastman has indicated in his excellent book on *The Enjoyment of Laughter*, you can do almost anything with a child or with an animal if you do it "in play." You can take away the child's candy, or take away the dog's

bone, if you do it "in play." But once allow yourself to grow
serious and grownup and lose the spirit of being "in play,"
a dark and nameless something settles over the child or the
animal. The game ceases and relations become strained.
Childhood would be a perfect idyll were it not for one thing,
and that is the tendency of children at times to fall "out of
play." The boys on the block are playing "cops and rob-
bers," for example. They are hiding behind the parked cars
and creeping around the corners of buildings, hunting each
other, with their toy guns or with their fingers gestured in
imitation of a gun. A head emerges around a corner and
someone shouts, "Bang! You're dead!" All has gone well
and gleefully up to this point. The zest of the game has been
thrilling. But now that head from around the corner doesn't
want to die, and argues with the one who is supposed to
have shot him, contending that he saw the other first and
shouted, "Bang!" and the other is really the one who is dead.
Now what was once play becomes argument and confusion
and the game may break up at this point.

Here is another instance: little Johnnie has received a
football for his birthday. He and his playmates are out
scrimmaging on the corner lot. An argument arises and
Johnnie takes his ball and goes home. The game ends. You
can't play if you lose the mood of play. But children love
the game so much that they adjust their squabbles quickly.
Being so near the mood of play all the time, they don't hold
grudges or resentments. But children grown tall, whom we call
adults, have lost this facility largely. Growing up generally
means growing away from the mood of play and the spirit
of childhood which can create the world as it wants it to be.
Adults lose the capacity of make-believe. And then because
their world is not what they want it to be they explain the
causes as due to enemies outside of themselves. Then they
proceed to fight these enemies. But it is all serious and

heavy and cynical. There is none, or at least little, of the spirit of the child in this drama of adult human life. But the adult is always trying to recover the mood of being "in play." He is always trying to be less serious and heavy and trying to make the game of life more of a game as he knows in his inmost heart it is and should be. But the trouble is the adult cannot get cooperation. All the peoples of the world would like to play the game of peace and brotherhood, but when some are in the mood of play others are not. It is a question of all getting into the same mood of play, or the same spirit of the game, at the same time.

The spirit would always find a way to peace if enough men would get into it. But we have seen that in practical affairs the spirit is always induced to flow in accordance with the thoughts and reasonings of the mind. The mind may talk of peace but may not believe in peace, and hence will not call forth the spirit of peace which alone can confirm and make peace. The famous Kellogg-Briand Pact, signed by fifteen nations in 1928, all agreeing to outlaw war as an instrument of national policy, is an outstanding example of the world of grownups which has lost the spirit of childhood. All of these nations tried to play the game of peace, but they were not "in play," and so the game never came off. They had a beautiful plan, but the spirit was never there to give it wings and animation. Within two or three years some of the signatories were taking their ball and going their own way.

Surely this is part of what Jesus has in mind in this telling parable. Grownups trying to play the game of peace and brotherhood among men are like children in the market place trying to play at funerals and weddings. They have a falling-out and then accuse each other of being wrong, and the game turns into a quarrel. A wedding and a funeral signify the extremes of human emotion. One is the brightest joy, the other is the darkest grief. One means parting, leaving and separation; the other means joining, union and atonement. These two elemental emotions are necessary in any creative achievement, in any new enterprise, or any new way of living. In order for man or nation to change, old patterns must be discarded, old ways of thinking and feeling must be given up, and this is painful. It is a form of death. And on the other side new modes of thinking and feeling must be aroused and wooed and accepted. The mind must be enthusiastic for the new and the better in the same sense that a pair who are betrothed are eager to be married. But in the ordinary life of the ordinary man these principles are lost sight of.

Most men believe in the goals of religion but they don't, generally speaking, marry those goals intellectually and emotionally, and at the same time give up those modes of thought and action which prevent the realization of the goals. And these two acts of the mind are absolutely necessary if we are really going to play the game and not merely pretend that we are playing. In the purely local setting of the parable this is all portrayed by Jesus' allusion to himself, to the teachings of John the Baptist, and to his own teaching. For John came calling on men to repent and change their ways of thinking. He came to pour dirty water out of the vessel of life, and Jesus came to pour in the clean. In this sense John and Jesus represent two modes of psychological motion necessary to progress. John is pictured as a hairy, rough man, dressed in rough garments, and his teaching was also rough, and its application painful. He spoke of putting the axe to the root of the tree. He represents that surgical kind of thinking which ruthlessly routs out erroneous concepts and cuts away the dead weight of the past.

But the Scribes and the Pharisees did not respond to John because they could not bear to change their ways of think-

ing. The Pharisees practiced religion in an external fashion.
They gave tithes of mint and anise and cumin, but as Jesus
says, "forgot the weightier matters of the law." They thought
that man was made for the Sabbath and not that the Sabbath was made for man. They stressed outer ritual and external performance. They believed that this gave merit and
goodness, just as Christians believed in the days immediately
before Luther came and announced anew that justification
was by faith. But the jungle grows up fast and every age
needs a new Luther to remind it that faith is the key to life.
That not what one does or says but what one is, is the cause
of one's experience.

So to a Pharisee or a believer in externals, in the time of
Jesus or now in our time, the preaching of John is without
effect. The modern Pharisee is the individual who emphasizes externals at the expense of internals. The great teachers of the race, and when not the great teachers then life
itself, always comes preaching, saying repent, cast away
these foolish thoughts, and accept the simple doctrine that
your faith can set you free. There is something wonderful
and grand inside of you which can take charge of your life
and organize it into patterns of wholeness and peace and
plenty. Cut away this deference to things and to externals.
Don't let your confidence depend upon the behavior of
someone else. And don't let your faith rest upon what someone else has done with the power of God in his life. If your
faith rests in someone else, even upon Jesus himself, there
is somewhat of weakness in it. It has an external point of
reference, and so long as this persists it bars the way to the
internal point of reference which opens the door to the kingdom of heaven.

So the perennial Pharisee is like a child standing in the
market place. Other children are engaging in a game, a fu-

neral for example, the game of loss, giving up, dissolution, and death of old forms and expressions. But the perennial Pharisee is stubborn in his own opinions. He will not enter into the game because he does not want to give up anything. He likes what he believes and he likes what he does. And to the call "come mourn with us," he turns a deaf ear. Like some children he would rather argue over the rules of the game than to play the game itself.

As John represents the giving up and cutting away of old and limited ways of thinking and acting, so Jesus represents the introduction of the new, the positive and the constructive way of faith. John is a faster; Jesus is a feaster. John precedes Jesus for the simple reason that the mind has to give up its wrong attitudes before it can enjoy good ones. The coming of Jesus into the human heart presupposes a previous visitation from John. When we have disabused our minds of the belief that something external is causing our misery, then we shall have rejoicing in ourselves alone over the simple truth that it is our faith that has made us free. But it is as hard to embrace the new as it is to give up the old. It is difficult for a mind and body schooled in the experience of illness to believe that such a simple thing as faith can heal the body. It is difficult for a person who has never made a go of any kind of business to accept the idea that a change of his thinking may make him a success. So the perennial Pharisee still stands on the street corner like the children, when Jesus comes preaching a positive, constructive philosophy of faith, when the new mind comes eating and drinking of new visions and possibilities in the kingdom of heaven.

And all of this again is reason why the publican and the harlot go into the kingdom of heaven ahead of the Scribes and Pharisees. For the Scribes and Pharisees are satisfied with themselves. They are not teachable. But the publican and the harlot have all to gain and nothing to lose. They know that the old game which they have been playing was not too much fun, so they are eager to try anything new.

We cannot leave this parable without pinpointing it to a very personal and individual application, and encouraging the reader to do this. In the individual mind John and Jesus are represented by two poles of psychological action. When you want health do not hold to the belief that a weakness you inherited in the blood from your parents is causing your illness. Get enough spiritual understanding so that you can reason this false concept away. From the standpoint of biology and the other physical sciences it may be true. But from the standpoint of the spiritual science, your inheritance is from God. If you have been tending to blame your misfortune and lack of success in life upon other people or groups, or situations and circumstances, try now to cut this out and cast it aside. There will be weeping and wailing and gnashing of teeth inside of you when you do this. It will cause pain, and at times you may find yourself in despair. But persevere and then swing to the other pole of your being and embrace the ideal of your desiring. Eat of it and feast upon it in prayer and meditation until, like a piece of physical food, you make it one with your own nature. When it is in you and you are in it, a new day will dawn for you, both in the health of body and the success of your affairs.

THE PARABLE OF THE CANDLE

Ye are the light of the world. A city that is set on an hill
cannot be hid.
  Neither do men light a candle, and put it under a
bushel, but on a candlestick; and it giveth light unto
all that are in the house.
Matthew 5:14-15

Parallel passages: Mark 4:2, Luke 8:16, also 11:33.

"YE ARE THE LIGHT of the world" is one of the most profound
statements ever made. It encompasses the best of twenty-
five centuries of philosophy and metaphysics as well as some
of the most basic concepts of the new physics. Metaphysics
has always seen the outside, external world as the projection
of states of mind. But with the coming of Einstein, physics,
too, began to note the relationship between observer and
reality. Lincoln Barnett, in his splendid volume for the layman, *The Universe and Dr. Einstein,* says, "Thus, gradually
philosophers and scientists arrived at the startling conclusion
that since every object is simply the sum of its qualities, and
since qualities exist only in the mind, the whole objective
universe of matter and energy, atoms and stars, does not
exist except as a construction of the consciousness, an edifice
of conventional symbols shaped by the senses of man."
  The awareness or light of the human mind determines
what it sees and experiences in the physical world. This is
true in several ways. It is true, first of all, in the fact that
the human eye is sensitive only to a narrow band of light or
radiation that falls between the red and the violet. Only
the difference of a few one hundred thousandths of a centi-
meter in wave lengths makes the difference between visibil-

ity and invisibility. The wave length of red light being
.00007 cm. and that of violet light .00004 cm. But on either
side of this narrow band are other kinds of radiation or light
from the sun. There are the well-known ultraviolet rays
which are too short for the human eye to perceive but which
we can record photographically. There are the infrared rays
which are too long to excite the retina to an impression of
light but which we can detect as heat upon the surface of
our skin. There are X-rays and cosmic rays and radio waves.
The human eye is blind to most of the "lights" in the world,
and of all the great reality that lies around him, man can see
only what comes within the range of this narrow band of
visible light. How different the world must appear or would
appear to a human being if his eye were as sensitive as
X-rays or infrared rays. Thus, for all of us, the experience
of the external world is limited by our allotment of light.
The world also assumes different aspects at twilight. Shapes
are distorted and forms are obscured. In the twilight, men
have been known to mistake a tree for a man or a mound of
earth for an animal. Under such conditions, the judgment is
distorted along with the visual image and the conclusions of
the mind are erroneous and faulty.

Crossing over the thin line that separates physics from
metaphysics, we perceive that the same principle operates.
The true spiritual light of the mind is understanding. We
speak of throwing light upon a dark and troublesome question or problem. We also speak of a person acting according
to his own light. New perceptions and illuminations con-
stitute the light in the mind. And the mind needs more and
more of these if it is to see its way clearly to its goals. But
sometimes the perceptions of the mind are a kind of a dark
light, a confused understanding. And Jesus says elsewhere
(Matthew 6:23) "If therefore the light that is in thee be
darkness, how great is that darkness!" The mind's stock of

information, its perceptions and its viewpoints and opinions, all of these form its light by which it takes its way among the sorrows and the joys, the successes and the failures of this world. If the light of the mind is dark and it believes that causation is outside of it, it peoples the outside world with all sorts of dangers. And then, by virtue of the fact that the mind itself is cause, it enters into an experience of that which itself projects. If the light or understanding of the mind is based upon the true observation of itself as cause, then this light extends into all the corners of the objective world, banishing the shadows and revealing good where formerly danger and evil were thought to dwell, lurking in the shadows. This very perception is in itself the light which Jesus speaks about.

It is to the disciples that he addresses this announcement, "Ye are the light of the world." Those minds which are trained and disciplined in spiritual thinking know that "I am the light of the world." When a person is aware of the principle of inner causation, he has a light. What shall he do with it? Shall he hide it, ignore it or fail to use it? Shall he allow the outside world with its strong suggestions of impotency and danger cover up the light of understanding? No, says Jesus. Rather, let your light shine. It is the light of the mind which determines whether you see confusion and limitation or whether you see order and abundance. When you are trying to see your way clear, don't allow the images of sense to becloud your vision. If through the light of your mind you can see possibilities beyond present conditions and facts, don't let the present conditions and facts dismay you or inhibit the movement of affirmative thought in you. Don't let them put a damper on your spirits. Don't let them cover up your true understanding of the mighty power of God in man. A city that is set on a hill cannot be hid. It announces its presence from miles away. The parable suggests that a person likewise should announce his spiritual presence with peace and poise, goodwill and power. "The spirit of man is the candle of the Lord," and its light reveals what the Lord or the power of life is doing in the individual sphere of existence.

When you know that creative power is within you, you have a light that enables you to see and to affirm the presence of all kinds of good which are not discernible to the ordinary mind. Hold this light aloft like a torch and walk in the path of its illumination. When conditions suggest loss or danger, you will know something beyond and above these. You will "endure as seeing him who is invisible." Like Job, you will know that His candle shines upon your head and by His light you walk through darkness. (Job 29:3)

5

IMPORTUNITY IN THE LAW

———————

THE PARABLE OF
THE IMPORTUNATE WIDOW

And he spake a parable unto them to this end, that men
ought always to pray, and not to faint;

Saying, There was in a city a judge, which feared
not God, neither regarded man:

And there was a widow in that city; and she came
unto him, saying, Avenge me of mine adversary.

And he would not for a while; but afterward he
said within himself, Though I fear not God, nor regard man;

Yet because this widow troubleth me, I will avenge
her, lest by her continual coming she weary me.

And the Lord said, Hear what the unjust judge
saith.

And shall not God avenge his own elect, which cry

day and night unto him, though he bear long with them?

I tell you that he will avenge them speedily. Nevertheless when the Son of man cometh, shall he find faith on the earth?

Luke 18:1-8

THE PARABLE OF
THE IMPORTUNATE FRIEND

And it came to pass, that, as he was praying in a certain place, when he ceased, one of his disciples said unto him, Lord, teach us to pray, as John also taught his disciples.

And he said unto them, When ye pray, say, Our Father which art in heaven, Hallowed be thy name. Thy kingdom come. Thy will be done, as in Heaven, so in earth.

Give us day by day our daily bread.

And forgive us our sins; for we also forgive every one that is indebted to us. And lead us not into temptation; but deliver us from evil.

And he said unto them, Which of you shall have a friend, and shall go unto him at midnight, and say unto him, Friend, lend me three loaves;

For a friend of mine in his journey is come to me, and I have nothing to set before him?

And he from within shall answer and say, Trouble me not: the door is now shut, and my children are with me in bed; I cannot rise and give thee.

I say unto you, Though he will not rise and give him, because he is his friend, yet because of his importunity he will rise and give him as many as he needeth.

And I say unto you, Ask, and it shall be given you; seek and ye shall find; knock, and it shall be opened unto you.

For every one that asketh receiveth; and he that seeketh findeth; and to him that knocketh it shall be opened.

If a son shall ask bread of any of you that is a father, will he give him a stone? or if he ask a fish, will he for a fish give him a serpent?

Or if he shall ask an egg, will he offer him a scorpion?

If ye then, being evil, know how to give good gifts unto your children: how much more shall your heavenly Father give the Holy Spirit to them that ask him?

Luke 11:1-13

PEOPLE USED TO SAY that the squeaking wagon wheel got the grease. And we still observe that the one who makes the most noise attracts attention to himself. In a crowd of shoppers at a busy counter, there is always one who thrusts herself forward volubly and gets the attention of the clerk. There is the salesman who rejoices in the fact that he made himself so much of a pest that he caused a man to buy something that he didn't want.

These are examples of how not to be persistent and persevering. For they are prime examples of how to get people to dislike you and build up enmity for yourself. Persistence always wins something in any world, and in this world we see many examples like those above. The student of the spiritual science will be careful how he uses his persistence and importunity, for he will recognize that the only thing he can ever win is the reaction to his own thoughts. Since this is true he will not persist in any thought or action which deprives another of his right, or in any way tends to harm another. To do so is to encourage the action of the law to backfire upon oneself. But persistence is always effectual, whether for good or for ill, and Jesus told these two parables to illustrate it.

The hungry friend at midnight who asks for bread and the aggrieved widow who insisted on justice from a judge illustrate how pure persistence sets the law of mind in motion, and give great force to the instruction of Jesus: "Ask, and it shall be given you; seek, and ye shall find; knock, and it shall be opened unto you." He follows this by assuring us that no one who really does ask and seek and knock will ever come away empty-handed. His counsel is as sure and as accurate and as infallible as that chemical law which causes water to be formed out of two gases in the ratio of two to one.

Because it is a law, it has nothing to do with goodness or with sentiment or with the brand of religion that you may practice. God is no respecter of persons. The law works the same for the bad man as for the good man. The sun shines upon the just as upon the unjust. If any man will persist in any effort he will achieve a result in confirmation of his thought and motivation. There is no morality in the law itself. The law is impartial and neutral. It is not concerned with ends. It is the means to all ends. Morality is concerned with how people use the law. The law is as responsive to the bad man as it is to the good man. The law takes a person's aim and desire and turns it into embodiment and function. Whether the result of a man's persistent aim is good or bad is inherent in the aim itself. Every man's thought carries its reward with it. To become good men, we must learn how to choose good ends. We must learn that good ends are the satisfaction of our own desires without any harm to anybody else. The law allows us to do this, indeed makes it possible for us to do this. Therefore, understanding of the law comes first and we must live with Moses before we can live with Jesus. The law came by Moses, but grace and truth came by Jesus Christ. Grace and truth are the right use of the law and the happy results obtained thereby. And Paul points out that: "Love is the fulfilling of the law." This means that when we have used the law correctly we shall find ourselves in a state of goodwill with all people. Ourselves feeling this way with others, and others feeling that way with us. This harmonious state of love or goodwill betokens that we have used the law correctly.

But the stark reality of the law is that persistence always wins out. The two parables illustrating this are from everyday life, and their truth is so apparent as to enable any one of us to find their counterparts in everyday modern life. Persistence is a truth in any realm, in any field, at any time. As Oliver Wendell Holmes observed,

> Be firm! One constant element of luck
> Is genuine, solid, old Teutonic pluck.
> Stick to your aim, the mongrel's hold will slip;
> But only crowbars loose the bulldog's grip.
> Small though he looks, the jaw that never yields
> Drags down the bellowing monarch of the fields.
> "A Rhymed Lesson"

But persistence in the kingdom of heaven with prayer is not quite the same as persistence in the rough and tumble affairs of the world. They are alike, and that is all the parable is meant to convey. The parables put no premium upon rudeness or pushiness or aggressiveness. They do not countenance the insistence upon your own selfish purpose ahead and at the expense of other people's good. They simply illustrate the quality and the effectiveness of being persistent. In true prayer you are not in competition with any one but your old self and its limited opinions, and it is all right, therefore, for you to push ahead of this self and relegate it to the background of your life and experience. There is no question in true prayer of persisting in any aim which blights another's life and which wins any kind of good which the other cannot claim also. The riches of the kingdom of heaven are so great and so infinite that there is no limitation on what any of us may desire and achieve.

So you are encouraged to insist on the good things for your life, to insist upon health and happiness, to insist upon divine right order and consummate beauty in your life, and to tolerate nothing less. You have no one to convince in prayer but yourself. The law of God is ready to give you your request the moment you "make known your requests with thanksgiving" and conviction. God has given all of his gifts of life and the enjoyment thereof to man. God has finished his works. We are now in the position of trying to realize this, and so in prayer we are persistently trying to open a larger area of our consciousness. It is not a question of the reluctance of the law to respond. "It is the Father's good pleasure to give you the kingdom." Realization and acceptance can come only through continued persistent attention to the soul's sincere desire.

As we have indicated, there is not always justice in ordinary life, but in the kingdom of heaven to which each person has appeal, there is always justice. For a person is always experiencing the exact reproduction of his own consciousness. A person is always under the orders of this tribunal and only this one. If a person's experience has been sad and full of limitation, he has a right at any time to make appeal to this higher court, and by reference to the law which grants all men all the good which they can receive and accept, he can begin to pray by thinking of an increased amount of good, recognizing it as his own, and persistently claiming it until his consciousness is impregnated with it. Then by the law of the mind his consciousness becomes his experience. Persistency wins in this world, and persistency wins in the kingdom of heaven. They are alike in this respect, as the two sides of the parable imply.

THE PARABLE OF
THE RICH MAN AND THE BEGGAR

There was a certain rich man, which was clothed in purple and fine linen, and fared sumptuously every day:

And there was a certain beggar named Lazarus, which was laid at his gate full of sores,

And desiring to be fed with the crumbs which fell from the rich man's table: moreover the dogs came and licked his sores.

And it came to pass, that the beggar died, and was carried by the angels into Abraham's bosom: the rich man also died, and was buried;

And in hell he lift up his eyes, being in torments, and seeth Abraham afar off, and Lazarus in his bosom.

And he cried and said, Father Abraham, have mercy on me, and send Lazarus, that he may dip the tip of his finger in water, and cool my tongue; for I am tormented in this flame.

But Abraham said, Son, remember that thou in thy lifetime receivedst thy good things, and likewise Lazarus evil things: but now he is comforted, and thou art tormented.

And beside all this, between us and you there is a great gulf fixed: so that they which would pass from hence to you cannot; neither can they pass to us, that would come from thence.

Then he said, I pray thee therefore, father, that thou wouldst send him to my father's house:

For I have five brethren; that he may testify unto them, lest they also come into this place of torment.

Abraham saith unto him, They have Moses and the prophets; let them hear them.

And he said, Nay, father Abraham: but if one went unto them from the dead, they will repent.

And he said unto him, If they hear not Moses and the prophets, neither will they be persuaded, though one rose from the dead.

Luke 16:19-31

WE MAY WITH PROFIT use this parable as a preachment and as a lesson against self-indulgence, selfishness and the improper uses of wealth. This parable also illustrates for us the great truth that all things are forever changing to their opposites. Is the sun shining? There will be clouds. Is it cloudy? The sun will shine. All material shapes and forms of matter are continually disintegrating to the formless, and out of the invisible, new forms and shapes are continually coming into view. Life's energy is not static but dynamic; always moving from some place to some other place, coming from somewhere, going somewhere. In physical science, we have what is called the law of the conservation of energy, which means that energy is indestructible. It manifests itself in a multitude of forms and is constantly changing its forms. But energy itself remains. In religion we call this something which comes and goes and yet remains, spirit. And God is spirit. And God is the Ever-living One. So death or extinc-

tion cannot be ascribed to God or to spirit. It is the continuing
element of all existence. Now, man is an individualization
of the universal spirit. And men have always made a distinction between the spirit of man and his body, so that
when the body disintegrates, they have reasoned, the spirit
is liberated and goes to another place to continue and to develop. If the individual has been wicked during his life in
the body, then the spirit will be consigned to hell or to a
place of torment, known to the Greeks as Hades and to the
Hebrews as Sheol. If the person were a good man, his spirit
would go to heaven, a place of bliss.

Now all of this is, in a way, quite true, but perhaps we
should say there are two ways in which it is true. For the
materialistic mind it is true in just the simple way we have
explained it here. It is difficult for such a mind to grasp the
concept that there is another very real world existing side
by side and interpenetrating the world of matter; this is the
world of mind and spirit in which we all live and move and
have our being. So the earth-mind materializes its heaven
and its hell and locates them in definite spatial boundaries.

It is against this materialistic background that the Parable
of the Rich Man and the Beggar is told. Dives, as the rich
man is called, traditionally, was not a bad man, but he was
a selfish man. I do not mean that he was selfish merely because he was not more mindful of the needs of the poor
beggar at his gate, but he was selfish because he was not
mindful of his own future. This is the higher meaning of the
parable. Jesus is telling this parable to the Pharisees, "who
were covetous." He is telling the parable as a warning
against those attitudes which covet external position and
wealth and neglect the inner wealth of the mind and the
spirit. The parable is a further warning against that attitude
which becomes so in love with its own condition and situation that it fails to grow. It tends to stop where it is and

build a permanent abode, to be dogmatic and final. It discards nothing and takes on nothing new. It is satisfied. It assumes that because everything is going well and it is surrounded in luxury, that all is well. It takes a sort of smug satisfaction in its own self-righteousness; "Ye are they which justify yourselves before men; but God knoweth your hearts: for that which is highly esteemed among men is abomination in the sight of God." You cannot be satisfied and rest on your laurels. Life demands that you grow and growth means preparation in your mind and your spirit for the next stage of your existence. The rich man in the parable is a symbol or a type of such a satisfied and self-centered, self-indulgent mind. The beggar, on the other hand, is an example of the type of mind which is conscious of its great need and which longs for fulfillment. Such a mind in spite of its present deplorable condition is growing. For its desiring and its longing are making deposits in the bank of consciousness upon which the mind will one day draw. Most of the energy of such a mind goes into its longing for better things, and so such a mind is sending life or energy ahead of it, so to speak, and this life or energy will collect and organize at a certain point in time and space and become the new habitation or existence of the mind. Psychologically and metaphysically speaking, this new existence is the "afterlife" of the mind.

In the finer meaning of the parable, as in the rest of the teachings of the Bible, heaven and hell are not necessarily places to which we go when we lay down the body. Heaven and hell may be experienced right here on earth while we are in the body. A mind that will not grow will be plunged into torment and the mind which longs for higher things will be granted them.

Lazarus and Dives are representatives of two kinds of thinking or two modes of feeling present in everyone of us.

There are two tendencies or possibilities in every human mind. If we follow the way of Dives, then we shall become satisfied with our present state, with the things of the world and the learning of the senses. We shall be rich in materialistic experiences and sense impressions. We shall be the prisoner of the senses, lost in our routine, involved in our present activities until we find it difficult to believe that there is or could be anything else than what we now know and experience. But because growth is a necessity forced upon us, life will have to bring us suffering in order to make us aware of its higher values and purposes, and then from the depth of our pain and our torment we shall cast our eyes upward to behold the higher levels of life and by contrasting them with our own condition, we shall learn to aspire and to grow. Thus, once more we shall get in line with life's constructive program. That part or phase of our life which we have accepted and about which we are satisfied is a possible source of trouble to us. It is leading us toward suffering in order to open our eyes to something higher. But there is a beggar in everyone of us, too. There is something in us which longs and craves and desires. It is humble and meek and receptive by necessity. It is the beggar at our gates, the gates of our mind. We must feed the beggars. That is, the rich must give attention to the discontentment, the aspiration, the undeveloped talent in oneself, lest these become repressed into the subconscious to cause us trouble later on.

Now the mind which gets into trouble by failing to aspire and to grow and is plunged into torment and discovers the true significance of its situation, often complains, "why didn't someone tell me these things?" Now it recognizes its mode of thinking and feeling and living to have been erroneous and that mode which is represented by Lazarus, the spiritual faculty in man is recognized to be the correct one. And the mind would have contact with Lazarus immediately.

Every mind has its spiritual faculty which it cannot wholly
lose, and when it is brought low into Hades, it can recognize
this spiritual faculty high in heaven or in a more exalted
and happier state. But Jesus points out that there is a great
gulf between the two. A mind which has lived in matter
and its laws all of its life cannot, overnight, understand the
realm of the spirit. People suppose that they can understand
something simply because it is told them. But this is not so.
The mind can only understand after preparation. The gulf
between Dives and Lazarus is not one of time and space.
It is one of mind and consciousness. It is one of understanding. That gulf is no wider, spatially, than the gulf between
two radio broadcasts which are entering your room at this
instant. The only thing that separates them is frequency.
There is a great gulf between spiritual thought and purely
worldly thought, and it takes preparation and growth and
living to move from one to the other. Therefore, one is in
torment in his own inward fire until such time as all of the
old kind of thinking is burned away and he sees the spiritual
truth, which, like gold, always abides without diminishing
after the fire has cooled.

But the mind which is in torment doesn't understand this
yet and thinks that it can understand if it were only told,
if things were only explained to it, and so it begs that someone be sent from this world of the shades to the five brethren
still on earth that they may be taught and warned to avoid
this predicament. In the higher meaning, the five brethren
represent the five senses. For while the inner self or soul is
in torment, the five senses of the mind are still in the world,
seeing, hearing, tasting, touching and feeling. Since most of
our knowledge comes through the five senses, we suppose
that if someone would only speak to us the right words
and show us the right pictures, explain the right path,
that we could understand. But spiritual understanding

does not come through the five senses. It comes through a combination of the five senses and the inner senses as we explained in the Parable of The Ten Virgins. In reading the sacred writings of the race and in meditating upon them, the mind is stimulated to inner illuminations and understandings and thus, in the parable, Abraham replies to Dives, "They have Moses and the Prophets; let them hear them."

But Dives is still unconvinced and, in the typical manner of the worldly mind, thinks that if something dramatic were done, then the mind would be so impressed as to understand. But spiritual thinking also knows the fallacy of this. The mind that is still enmeshed in worldly thought and in sense perception will be impressed for a few hours by one rising from the dead. But it will presently slip back into its own established patterns of thought. I have seen such minds gain the most remarkable answers to prayer only to have them explain away the results in terms of matter and phenomena. We cannot maintain any position to which we have not ascended in consciousness. And so the Parable of the Rich Man and the Beggar teaches essentially the same lesson as Omar the Tentmaker when he says,

> I sent my Soul through the Invisible,
> Some letter of that After-life to spell:
>   And by and by my Soul return'd to me
>   And answer'd, "I Myself am Heav'n and Hell:"

6

SKILL AND FORESIGHT IN
APPLYING THE LAW

THE PARABLE OF
THE UNRIGHTEOUS STEWARD

And he said also unto his disciples, There was a certain
rich man, which had a steward; and the same was ac-
cused unto him that he had wasted his goods.

And he called him, and said unto him, How is it
that I hear this of thee? give an account of thy stewardship; for thou mayest be no longer steward.

Then the steward said within himself, What shall
I do? for my lord taketh away from me the stewardship: I cannot dig; to beg I am ashamed.

I am resolved what to do, that, when I am put out
of the stewardship, they may receive me into their
houses.

So he called every one of his lord's debtors unto

him, and said unto the first, How much owest thou unto my lord?

And he said, An hundred measures of oil. And he said unto him, Take thy bill, and sit down quickly, and write fifty.

Then said he to another, And how much owest thou? And he said, An hundred measures of wheat. And he said unto him, Take thy bill, and write fourscore.

And the lord commended the unjust steward, because he had done wisely: for the children of this world are in their generation wiser than the children of light.

And I say unto you, Make to yourselves friends of the mammon of unrighteousness; that, when ye fail, they may receive you into everlasting habitations.

He that is faithful in that which is least is faithful also in much; and he that is unjust in the least is unjust also in much.

If therefore ye have not been faithful in the unrighteous mammon, who will commit to your trust the true riches?

And if ye have not been faithful in that which is another man's, who shall give you that which is your own?

No servant can serve two masters: for either he will hate the one, and love the other; or else he will hold to the one, and despise the other. Ye cannot serve God and mammon.

Luke 16:1-13

THIS HAS OFTEN been considered a difficult parable, but it is actually not so. It follows the uncompromising line of all of the rest of the parables and of Jesus' teaching in general.

That uncompromising line is this: there is a law which governs human experience. That law may be either a law of bondage or a law of liberty for the individual. Whichever it is, is determined by what the person thinks and how he thinks within himself. All judgment is given unto the son and with what judgment ye judge ye shall be judged, with what measure ye mete it shall be meted to you again. Therefore, a person has nothing to work with save his own thought, and the correction of every outward difficulty lies in the correction of one's own thought. The promotion of one's estate is through the promotion of one's thoughts to a higher level of consciousness.

For you, as a human being, are a steward of a great estate. That estate is the realm of mind or consciousness, and the way you work and give account of yourself in that estate determines every other factor and quality in your experience of things past, things present and things to come. As we have seen, you cannot just let your mind go. Without supervision the mind becomes the habitation of devils and demons. Just as an empty house becomes the habitation of rodents and spiders and cobwebs and dust and decay in general, an empty house also attracts thieves and despoilers. (See Matthew 12:43-45) A person must supervise his thinking and establish right concepts in the mind so that the law will work through these as a law of liberty. One should learn to be as astute and wise and careful with his mind as he is with his money, and it is these two basic concepts and values, one a material one and one a spiritual one, which are laid side by side to form the parallel in this parable.

We have the story of a steward, or a foreman, or an overseer, and his shrewd cunning in handling material wealth. And alongside of this, for the studied consideration of the spiritual businessman, is the concept that the disciple in the kingdom of heaven should also be shrewd and wise and

even cunning in handling the treasure of mind and consciousness itself. So let us look at the outermost story first
and then at its spiritual analogue next. It is an account of a
sharp-witted rascal who "feathered his own nest" at the
expense of his employer. As such it is no different from a half-
dozen other stories you might read every week in the newspaper about modern business life. This fellow was a smart
operator, for he got himself out of a very difficult situation.
He thought and reasoned and then acted his way out of it,
all in terms and acts of unrighteousness, to be sure, nevertheless sagacious and successful. And his lord or employer
commended him for his wisdom. That doesn't mean that he
condoned his actions and allowed him to continue in his
employ. He fired him forthwith, but he did acknowledge
that the steward was a sharp operator. The steward made
use of the goods and the business he was in charge of to
make friends for himself, so that when he would be out of a
job there would be contacts and friends to aid him. He did
not reduce the debts of his employer's tenants because he
was interested in their welfare. He was interested in his
own. He did the tenants a favor that he might secure their
favor. In other words, he anticipated life, and with foresight and with shrewd judgment prepared for eventualities.

His kind is everywhere, in politics and in business. Now,
Jesus obviously told the parable to encourage religious peo-
ble to be more sagacious in their handling of spiritual
matters. But particularly, the parable implies with great
forcefulness, that a person should be wise and shrewd in the
handling of his own inner life. For man has business in two
worlds, the world of the mind and the world of things. The
average man is much smarter in dealing with the world of
things than he is in dealing with his own mind, and therefore
Jesus observed that the children of this world are wiser in
their generation than the children of light. For the children

of light are those spiritually minded people who have perceived that the things of the mind determine the things of
the flesh, or the things of the eye and the hand. They therefore have perception and light. But they are often very ineffective in making use of that perception. They may still
be afraid to put their trust in pure consciousness alone. They
are overawed by circumstances and people and situations,
and too easily swayed by the turn of events. They are sen-
timental and idealistic, but naïve and impractical. Sometimes they are like the Pharisees of Jesus' time. They mouth
platitudes, engage in all of the external practices of religion,
and then assume that they are at the head of the line for
heaven. We have already observed how Jesus noted that the
publicans and the harlots went into the kingdom of heaven
before the Pharisees. Hence there was something wrong
with their religion. It was ineffective. The trouble with the
children of light through all the ages is that they see far
more than they can do. Until the rise of psychology, Christianity had consistently overlooked the fact of the subconscious or the unconscious side of man. And this had reduced
its effectiveness. This is true not only of Christianity but of
religions in general.

When you announce an ideal such as the religious ideal
expressed in the commandment, Love thy neighbor as thyself, you must be prepared to meet the opposition to that
ideal which exists in your own subconscious or underworld.
For everything comes in pairs in this world. There is no
idea of good without its opposite idea of evil or denial of
that good. For every positive affirmation there is a negative
denial. When the religious sense announces an ideal such
as love thy neighbor, the outer senses immediately deny it,
because love of neighbor is not a condition which is generally prevalent in the world where the outer senses are in at-
tendance. Now this denial or opposition or error must be

handled by the mind which announces the ideal, and if it is not handled effectively then the ideal becomes weak and ineffective. In the subconscious of every person, whether religious or not, lie many denials of the ideal life. The subconscious is the seat of the emotions and therefore the powerhouse of man. If an idea is subconscious, then it is regnant and ruling and automatic. It has authority to act. It compels the individual to action. Therefore if a person wants to get his ideal into action, he must get the cooperation of his own subconscious mind. But if his own subconscious is already possessed by another, then he has to face that opposition and overcome it.

Jesus points this out quite clearly in his argument with the Pharisees related in the twelfth chapter of Matthew, and ending with the comment that one cannot enter into a strong man's house and spoil his goods except he first bind the strong man and then he will spoil his house. The subconscious is the strong man, and the spiritual thinker who is going to be really effective in realizing his ideals and desires, in discharging the duties of his religion, and in extending the kingdom of heaven upon earth beginning with his own life, must first of all take control of his own unconscious. He must destroy the negative or the shadow life which binds it in bondage, which often compels him to do things which he does not want to do, and causes him to refrain from doing the things which he knows he ought to do. The practice of the religion of Jesus is not child's play. It is not sentimentality or idealism only. It is these plus right reason, keen perception, sagacity and shrewdness in the extreme. One must learn to see that certain negative things are in control of his own powerhouse to regain that control.

Now the law as it is taught in the Bible, that is the law of the mind, has for its basic principle the understanding of the singleness of creative power. Reasoning from this prin-

ciple, the spiritual thinker develops real strength in addition
to idealism. He takes charge of his own unconscious and
releases the power which is necessary to realize his ideals.
So the spiritual life in the kingdom of heaven calls for as
much shrewdness in its sphere as people in the worldly life
display in their sphere. When Jesus sends forth his disciples
he cautions them to be wise as serpents and harmless as a
dove. The unjust steward in the parable is wise as a serpent,
but he is not harmless as a dove, for he has robbed his employer of his goods and substance, and thereby has placed
himself under the reaction of the law of his own thought.

The spiritual workman is just as wise, ideally speaking,
but he does not think and act in any way such as will build
up negative reactions to the law. A spiritual thinker recognizes that he is a steward over the vast domain of consciousness which belongs to his Father in heaven. He is working
his particular vineyard or area of that consciousness. He
owns nothing in that estate. All is loaned to him. We do not
create consciousness, we modify it and develop it. Consciousness is the awareness of something which is infinite.
It is our lord, and it frequently demands an accounting from
us in the way of results and manifestations of our ideals.
The righteous steward governs his own mind wisely. His
confidence is not in things material but in his concept of the
one power, and his convictions that thoughts are things.

That brings us to this word "mammon" in the parable. It
means literally, confidence, but traditionally it means confidence in material forms of wealth; that means money
and goods and properties and lands and stocks and bonds
and so forth. These are the things that represent wealth
and security and power to the worldly minded person.
And he puts his confidence in these. He struggles for these
and develops shrewdness and cunning in acquiring them.
Neither the parable nor any of the teaching of the Bible

considers these things as bad in themselves. What the parable means by the unrighteous mammon is the confidence that misguided minds place in the material forms of wealth. To the person who believes "money will buy anything," the one necessity is to struggle for money and worldly wealth. This develops greed, one of the cardinal sins. Greed is excessive desire, and excessive desire is bad because it steals from the one who is excessive in his desire. That final piece of gold the miser grasps and places upon his already full cornucopia turns the whole thing to dust. So the word mammon has also come to mean avarice or excessive desire or greed for the forms of wealth. Thus avarice, or excessive desire, or misguided confidence in the material forms of wealth, is not a friend to man. It may seem at first sight to be a friend because excessive desire can gather much goods around it, but it is a false friend. In the end it will fail. The parable urges you to "make to yourselves friends of the mammon of unrighteousness; that, when ye fail, they may receive you into everlasting habitations." What kind of friends are these we must make? Are they friends such as the unjust steward made? No, that is only the analogy. We all have some desire for the worldly forms of wealth and some confidence in them, but we must guard against the desire and the confidence becoming excessive. We must cultivate the conviction that all external forms of wealth are but the expression and the projection of states of consciousness. Therefore our first confidence must be in the consciousness which causes the external manifestation, and not in the external things themselves.

If you look upon all forms of material wealth as the outward expression of your states of consciousness, then those outer forms are always your friends because your confidence is rightly placed and you are in accord with divine law and order, and are keeping a balance between the spiritual and the material. But if you look upon the external forms of wealth as things to be desired in themselves, apart from any development in consciousness, then you are off center, out of order, and the material forms of wealth will not give you what you seek. They will prove to be traitors in the end. They cannot be your friends. The unjust steward indeed has made himself friends, and when he loses his job he will have friends to go to who will loan him something in appreciation of his past favors. But he is a thief in his heart. He has lost his integrity. He has lost his character. And in the measure that he has lost these, he has lost all. For everything he turns his hand to will have something of error in it until he redeems and corrects this condition in himself and makes amends for his wrongdoing.

I said that you were the steward of a vast estate, meaning your own consciousness. But speaking more precisely it is your philosophy, or religion, or viewpoint and beliefs which is the steward in your own mind. If your basic philosophy is built upon confidence in external causation and in external forms of wealth, then you are making enemies of these, the mammon of unrighteousness. They will fail you some time, and when they fail you will have nowhere to turn. So study the laws of the kingdom of heaven, namely your own mind in its higher reaches, processes and possibilities. It is a very subtle parallel that the parable suggests between the way of the world and the way of the mind. It is easy to make the mistake that many students and commentators on this parable have made, namely, to suggest that money and properties are mammon. They are not. There is nothing good or bad in money of itself. Nor in stocks and bonds and houses and lands. They are completely neutral. But the way we use them determines good or evil for ourselves and for others. Therefore the mammon of unrighteousness is the misplaced confidence that human beings put in material acquisitions.

Jesus is unequivocal in pointing out that you cannot serve both God and mammon. God means the true cause, the spiritual sovereignty of spiritual ideas and moods. If you serve and worship these as the great truths of your life, resting in the absolute and unerring confidence that these will precipitate themselves by their own power and mechanics into objective correspondence, and if at the same time you relegate the corresponding conditions to the realm of secondary causation and effect, then you are truly worshiping God and putting the righteous mammon, or wealth, or confidence first. By building up this confidence in the consciousness, you make friends for all the future, and indeed for all eternity, so that when material things fail "they may receive you into everlasting habitations."

THE PARABLE OF
THE UNMERCIFUL SERVANT

Then came Peter to him, and said, Lord, how oft shall my brother sin against me, and I forgive him? till seven times?

Jesus saith unto him, I say not unto thee, Until seven times: but, Until seventy times seven.

Therefore is the kingdom of heaven likened unto a certain king, which would take account of his servants.

And when he had begun to reckon, one was brought unto him, which owed him ten thousand talents.

But forasmuch as he had not to pay, his lord commanded him to be sold, and his wife, and children, and all that he had, and payment to be made.

The servant therefore fell down, and worshipped him, saying, Lord, have patience with me, and I will pay thee all.

Then the lord of that servant was moved with compassion, and loosed him, and forgave him the debt.

But the same servant went out, and found one of his fellowservants, which owed him an hundred pence: and he laid hands on him, and took him by the throat, saying, Pay me that thou owest.

And his fellowservant fell down at his feet, and besought him, saying, Have patience with me, and I will pay thee all.

And he would not: but went and cast him into prison, till he should pay the debt.

So when his fellowservants saw what was done, they were very sorry, and came and told unto their lord all that was done.

Then his lord, after that he had called him, said unto him, O thou wicked servant, I forgave thee all that debt, because thou desiredst me:

Shouldest not thou also have had compassion on thy fellowservant, even as I had pity on thee?

And his lord was wroth, and delivered him to the tormentors, till he should pay all that was due unto him.

So likewise shall my heavenly Father do also unto you, if ye from your hearts forgive not every one his brother their trespasses.

Matthew 18:21-35

OF ALL THE SKILLS which the spiritual workman or the follower of Christ must learn and develop, none is more delicate, nor more important, nor more productive, than the skill of forgiveness. I speak of it as a skill because that is what it is in relation to the law. Real forgiveness is based upon a clear knowledge of the mathematical precision of the law of the mind. Of course some people forgive easily by nature. In this regard they are noble from their birth. But the average one of us, after exposure to the tensions and the grievances that arise in association with his fellows, must learn how to forgive. The supreme expression and example of forgiveness is made by the dying Christ upon the cross: "Father, forgive them for they know not what they do." And all true forgiveness is based upon the understanding that men who wrong their fellows do not know what they do.

A person who resents and hurts and tries to exact vengeance on others does not know what he is doing—to himself. If he did, he would soon take measures to correct his attitudes and actions. He is postulating a second cause, and placing an abomination in the temple where God, the first cause, alone should dwell, in sanctified oneness. The man who flies off the handle and gets angry with his brother is a victim of his own emotions, emotions which he has previously set loose by his own thinking, conscious or unconscious. He does not know this so he is somewhat in the position of a child who has been spoiled and allowed to indulge in tantrums. Such a man is not his own man. Such a person is like the demoniac or mad boy whose father described him to Jesus in these words: "And, lo, a spirit taketh him, and he suddenly crieth out; and it teareth him that he foameth again, and bruising him hardly departeth from him." (Luke 9:39) Emotions which have previously been set loose by destructive thinking can arise on certain unforeseen and unpredictable occasions and tear a man apart, and make him be uncivil with his neighbors and even violent to the point of murder. When we recognize that such an one is not under his own conscious control, that he does not know what he is doing, it tempers the harshness of our judgment and helps us to forgive him, just as a parent is helped to forgive a child because the parent understands the child is not yet under the control of its own reason, or under the control of true insights and perceptions.

And you can afford to forgive others when you know the spiritual law, for no others can hurt you. When you predicate loss or hurt or gain or good upon the actions of others or upon things, you are actually stealing something from yourself. You are denying the action of the one spiritual power in your life, and therefore limiting yourself to small realizations and experiences. If, on the other hand, you know the singleness of the power and that it is mind or consciousness, and because you think, it is in you, and that therefore you are equipped to accept all the blessings life holds for you irrespective of what other people do or do not do, then you can get other people out of your hair, and off your shoulders, and abolish all reasons for resentment. Real forgiveness by you of another is changing your own thought and bringing it into line with the divine law. When you resent another you are either secretly wishing him harm, or at least believing that he is worthy of harm. When you forgive, you change your thought on this matter and realize that no other person is ever the cause of harm or limitation in your life. If you have been hurt or cheated and another was the instrument, you realize that the other was an instrument of your own consciousness. Your consciousness is cause, and your own thinking or lack of thinking allowed this limitation or hurt to happen to you. When you forgive you change this line of thought and reaffirm your divine right to all things good, and reassert your conscious claim to them. Thus you get the other fellow out of your mind and you waste no energy in thinking of him as a cause of trouble in your life. In forgiving, you are not so much doing the other fellow a favor as you are doing yourself a favor. This is precisely the reason for the injunction to practice forgiveness seventy times seven. The moment you reassert your conscious claim to the good things of life irrespective of what other people do or do not do, or have done or have not done, then life, or the law, honors your claim. The law holds no grudge. It forgives. It forgives on the scientific basis, and by means of the scientific principle, that it automatically reverses its action toward you when you reverse your thought toward it. Thus it makes no difference how many times you have been in error or sin, the law does not hold it against you once you have changed and returned to a constructive, spiritual view of things. It is in this sense that God forgives man continuously and forever.

Religion means going back to God in everything and about everything, and God leaves that path open always no matter how many times we may wander away from it. He never closes the door. No matter how many mistakes we make, the law of God responds immediately the moment we do the thing right. It does not punish us for our mistake, merely allows us to experience the lack of what we desired and worked for. But it stands over us all in merciful patience, waiting for our understanding to clear. But if our understanding gets hung up on the air that other people have harmed us, or cheated us, or betrayed us, or in any way obstructed our health and happiness, and we allow this to engender bitter feelings in ourselves against these other people, then we have stepped off the spiritual path of God. We have turned our backs on the divine forgiveness and shut ourselves off from the heavenly mercy. We are in torment, but there can be no amelioration or change for us until we get a new viewpoint about our neighbor. When we change our thought about the man we hated and see that he is no cause of any of our harm, and we return to the acknowledgment of the one true spiritual cause within our own nature, then we are back on the path, we are in the divine favor once more, and the mercy that is thrice blessed, falleth as a gentle rain from heaven.

In the parable the kingdom of heaven is likened unto a certain king "which would take account of his servants. And when he had begun to reckon, one was brought unto him, which owed him ten thousand talents." Ten thousand talents was a lot of money. It is estimated to have been equal to about two million of our dollars. To anyone but a millionaire, therefore, it is a debt almost impossible to pay, and nearly all commentators have seen in this a symbol of our human debt to God which is so large that we cannot foresee the time when we shall have discharged it all. Yet we are, as Paul says, debtors to the whole law, and the great prayer formula given by Jesus in the Sermon on the Mount, reads this way: "Forgive us our debts as we forgive our debtors." What are our debts? Well, God, or the infinite being, has granted us life. Something has been paid into us, and we are all under obligation to pay it out. Circulation is the life of trade, and it is the life of man. It is the life of any organism, for when circulation stops, life stops. Another way of putting it is to say that energy has been bequeathed us, and energy is continually flowing into us, and what comes in must go out. Physical science points out how the sun keeps all life upon the earth going. Were it to withdraw too far in the winter time we should all die for want of warmth, which is life. And the mysterious cosmic rays which beat out of interstellar space upon our earth are other evidences of life that is streaming hitherward. We are indeed debtors to something. We are beholden. We are under obligation. We are stewards of a vast and a mighty force. We have to discharge our debt by passing on this life force to everything within our world. God has granted us life. We in turn must grant life to all things that come within the range of our attention.

First of all, this means our ideals that rise in the mind, as impulses, yearnings, urgings and desires. They are the seeds and the germs of life on this plane, and we by our assurance, our confidence, our faith, are able to grant them life by our constructive reception and thought about them. But the negative-minded man does not grant life to these inner urgings of the spirit. He meets them with doubt and with unreceptive attitudes, so that they lie like beggars at the gate of the rich man's table, feeding only upon the crumbs that fall from the master's table. Those things which could bless the negative person's life in terms of health, success and happiness, he starves by his refusal to admit them into life, the life of his mind and consciousness. And then, in order to explain the limitation in his life, he looks around him and lands upon another human being, perverts the stream of life which was given to him in purity, and filling it with the poison of his resentment and his hate, turns it upon another. And so long as he maintains this attitude and spends his energies in fuming at another, he will have nothing left for constructive purposes, and so will dig his own hole of sorrow deeper. Only when he understands the law of all this and recognizes that all the good of life is his by right of consciousness, and that no other person can mar this right, or withhold its full expression—only then will the person feel magnanimous and big enough to grant his former enemy the right to life, to liberty and the pursuit of happiness. The moment he does this, he is paying off his obligation to life. He is passing on the precious stuff of life, and he comes into a psychological agreement with the law, which is described as God forgiving him because he has forgiven his neighbor. It is simply impossible for you to get what you want while you tie up your emotions in resentment or hate. And that is why the law is explicit: forgive, and ye shall be forgiven.

We are all like the servant in the parable. We have all been forgiven by life. All our shortcomings, sins and mistakes are immediately as nothing when we change and acknowledge the law as dominant in our psychological and our external lives. But if then we act like the servant in the parable and do not forgive others, we immediately shut off the benefit of the infinite and divine forgiveness toward ourselves. Again, I say, life has granted us life, and it is our duty to pass it on and to grant everything and everyone else life. Grant every person his right to be himself. Grant him his right to be peculiar and eccentric and unconventional. Grant him his right to be different from you. God sends his rain and his sun upon the just and the unjust. Work and live to be equally generous with your portion, then you will be in tune with the great law.

THE PARABLE OF THE TWO DEBTORS

And one of the Pharisees desired him that he would eat with him. And he went into the Pharisee's house, and sat down to meat.

And, behold, a woman in the city, which was a sinner, when she knew that Jesus sat at meat in the Pharisee's house, brought an alabaster box of ointment,

And stood at his feet behind him weeping, and began to wash his feet with tears, and did wipe them with the hairs of her head, and kissed his feet, and anointed them with the ointment.

Now when the Pharisee which had bidden him saw

it, he spake within himself, saying, This man, if he were a prophet, would have known who and what manner of woman this is that toucheth him: for she is a sinner.

And Jesus answering said unto him, Simon, I have somewhat to say unto thee. And he saith, Master, say on.

There was a certain creditor which had two debtors: the one owed five hundred pence, and the other fifty.

And when they had nothing to pay, he frankly forgave them both. Tell me therefore, which of them will love him most?

Simon answered and said, I suppose that he, to whom he forgave most. And he said unto him, Thou hast rightly judged.

And he turned to the woman, and said unto Simon, Seest thou this woman? I entered into thine house, thou gavest me no water for my feet: but she hath washed my feet with tears, and wiped them with the hairs of her head.

Thou gavest me no kiss: but this woman since the time I came in hath not ceased to kiss my feet.

My head with oil thou didst not anoint: but this woman hath anointed my feet with ointment.

Wherefore I say unto thee, Her sins, which are many, are forgiven; for she loved much: but to whom little is forgiven, the same loveth little.

Luke 7:36-47

HERE IS A STORY dramatically portraying the prophecy that the publicans and harlots go into the kingdom of heaven before you. Jesus is at dinner at the house of a Pharisee, the living symbol of all religious materialism. The proud Phari-

see is obviously not overimpressed with the stature and the
dignity of his guest; in fact, he is not much impressed at all,
otherwise he would not have forgotten those small items of
hospitality which the Oriental mind is most diligent to observe. The way you treat your guest shows what you think
of him, and Simon certainly didn't treat Jesus very well. But
the harlot from the streets came in, she whom the Pharisee
disdained and despised, and poured out her whole heart of
love and devotion and recognition.

It takes a sense of need and limitation to make one aspire
and grow. Self-righteousness, self-satisfaction, unteachabil-
ity and self-willfulness are the great barriers to progress in
all human lives. Life places us all upon the highway, the
king's highway which goes by the mountaintops and not
through the valleys (Numbers 20:17), but we wander down
into the lower elevations. When a human life has taken such
a course it often has to descend to the lowest and darkest
valley before it can see the stars which will guide it back
to the highway of life. Every alcoholic who has become
sober will know what I mean, for he has been brought low
and had to acknowledge that he had no power by his will
alone over his own problem. He acknowledged something
higher, and it raised him up. The mind which has reached
extremity has nowhere to go but up, and in its extremity
and out of its great need, it aspires and reaches for something
higher. It has all to gain and nothing to lose.

This parable is a fine figure of the human mind whose
intellectual life is pharisaical, and whose emotional life is a
harlot. As we have seen, the Pharisee is a believer in external
form and practice. He does not go within. He is proud of
his knowledge. He is absolute and dogmatic in his beliefs.
He works for, and accepts, the praise of men in place of the
praise of the God of his own soul. He would rather be
thought good than be good. In his own estimation, he has

arrived. By his own standards, he is righteous, all others are sinners. Thus, speaking more psychologically and metaphysically, any human mind which is dogmatic, inflexible, unteachable and wrapped up with its beliefs in externals to the exclusion of the law of the mind and of the spirit, is like Simon the Pharisee. The saviour principle within every human mind is the creative power of its own thought—the divine word, which is at every beginning, which is with God, and is God, the creator. But the mind which is confirmed in its own external beliefs cannot appreciate this, so it is not very hospitable and receptive to the Saviour. It is like a host who invites a well-known personage to dinner out of curiosity, but not out of real appreciation. This kind of a proud, stuffed and unyielding mind brings its owner to great misery and sorrow, for it holds him away from future good. The action of the creative word is through the feeling, and this kind of a mind will not feel. It dismisses the feeling as relatively unimportant. It emphasizes intellect and knowledge, and therefore the feelings of such a mind, unregarded, unappreciated and unwatched, tend to wander and to play the harlot. Feelings must unite with something, and when the mind fails to provide true concepts for them to unite with, they join with false ones, and thus the emotional self, or the woman in each one of us, is said, in Biblical terms, to be a harlot.

When this state of things has brought the mind into misery and suffering, it is ready to acknowledge its own errors. But it is the feelings in the heart which change first. Slowly the proud spirit changes, and in desperation and great yearning it turns back and searches for the true saviour, and all real earnestness of seeking is repaid by the discovery of the creative principle within the mind itself. This discovery neutralizes all past errors, or, "thy sins which were scarlet shall become white as snow."

THE PARABLE OF THE GOOD SAMARITAN

And, behold, a certain lawyer stood up, and tempted him, saying, Master, what shall I do to inherit eternal life?

He said unto him, What is written in the Law? how readest thou?

And he answering said, Thou shalt love the Lord thy God with all thy heart, and with all thy soul, and with all thy strength, and with all thy mind; and thy neighbour as thyself.

And he said unto him, Thou hast answered right: this do, and thou shalt live.

But he, willing to justify himself, said unto Jesus, And who is my neighbour?

And Jesus answering said, A certain man went down from Jerusalem to Jericho, and fell among thieves, which stripped him of his raiment, and wounded him, and departed, leaving him half dead.

And by chance there came down a certain priest that way: and when he saw him, he passed by on the other side.

And likewise a Levite, when he was at the place, came and looked on him, and passed by on the other side.

But a certain Samaritan, as he journeyed, came where he was: and when he saw him, he had compassion on him,

And went to him, and bound up his wounds, pouring in oil and wine, and set him on his own beast, and brought him to an inn, and took care of him.

And on the morrow when he departed, he took

out two pence, and gave them to the host, and said
unto him, Take care of him; and whatsoever thou
spendest more, when I come again, I will repay thee.

Which now of these three, thinkest thou, was
neighbour unto him that fell among the thieves?

And he said, He that shewed mercy on him. Then
said Jesus unto him, Go, and do thou likewise.

Luke 10:25-37

LOVE, says St. Paul, is the fulfilling of the law. This can only
mean that when a person has seen and understood the law
and has set it into motion in his own life, and has fulfilled
it, then the state of that person's mind and consciousness
can only be characterized by the word love. He is in a state
of goodwill with himself, with all others, and with all things
and processes in the world. He is at peace with himself and
with all else. Nothing mars his composure. "Great peace
have they who love thy law, and nothing shall offend them."

We have seen that to love the law is to experience its corresponding action in ourselves. The law can be said to love
us, or love through us, in goodwill toward all other people.
This principle can be readily discerned by observing any
happy, well-integrated person. The person who is happy in
himself, well disposed toward all of his parts, inwardly and
outwardly, is most tolerant and magnanimous in his deal-
ings with others. A happy person carries no chips on his
shoulder. He is not easily insulted. He is extremely tolerant
and generous. Being conscious of his own great riches he is
charitable toward others.

This is the great lesson of this parable which the world
seems somehow to forget at almost every turn. We would
be good, but we can't be good because we do not fulfill the
law. We would love, but instead we find prejudice and hate
intervening because we have not observed the law of our

own minds and souls and fulfilled it within ourselves. We sincerely speak of brotherhood, but somehow in spite of ourselves we pass by on the other side. It is because we are not in control of our own inner life, and therefore we cannot do what we wish to do, and we cannot refrain from doing what we find ourselves compelled to do by the existence of our inner dictator. We are powerless in all of these respects until we learn the law of our own being and follow it to its conclusion or fulfillment. Then we shall find ourselves in that love which is the fulfilling of the law.

Who is my neighbor? It was a lawyer, who was supposed to know the law, who asked Jesus such a question. Jesus asked him what was written in the law, and how he read it. "And he answering said, Thou shalt love the Lord thy God with all thy heart, and with all thy soul, and with all thy strength, and with all thy mind; and thy neighbour as thyself." This is a summary of the ten commandments.* The first part of the lawyer's answer, "Thou shalt love the Lord thy God," is a summary of the first five commandments, all of which relate to the inner life of man and are enjoinders or reminders to everyone to estimate the immaterial power of thought and mind and consciousness as primal and supreme in all things. With this recognition of the law of the mind working in all things, the individual is freed from his fears and from his tensions, prejudices and resentments.

And the second part of the law, the summary of the second five commandments, follows as a matter of course, namely, the love of one's neighbor. But the mind that has not seen the law in its inward parts but still believes that the law is some rule of outer conduct, will quibble over fine points such as the lawyer is doing in the story. He has not seen the law in its inward parts. He is aware of men's differing views about questions of who is my neighbor. The Greek thought

* See *Ten Words That Will Change Your Life.*

every foreigner a barbarian. To the Jew the stranger was a
Gentile dog. And the Mohammedan thought of every alien
as an infidel. And still today, wherever men divide into
groups, whether over politics, religion, business, or nation-
ality, there is a strong tendency to favor a member of the
group above a stranger. But the parable points up the fact
that the true neighbor is whomever you come upon, whomever you meet first, wherever you meet him. Wherever anyone is in need, he is your neighbor.

But this is a parable, and therefore it not only illustrates
a truth on the external side of life, but it illustrates a spiritual
truth. From the standpoint of our inner life, then, who is
our neighbor? The thing that is closest to us, the concept or
idea in the mind which we meet first, when we come out of
our own secret chamber, that thought in the mind which
attracts us first and holds our attention longest, is our neighbor, mentally speaking. And if we do right by this neighbor
in the mind, we shall not find ourselves in much error in
regard to our physical neighbors.

As you go back and forth within your own mind, you will
find on occasion certain ideals and hopes and dreams and
projects which have fallen among the thieves. That is, they
have fallen among doubts and tensions and fears and prejudices. And these have stripped them of their vitality,
stripped them of their garments and wounded them. What
will you do? Pass by on the other side like the priest and
the Levite? These are the representatives of external religion. They can do no other than pass by on the other side.
Only the awareness of the creative law can give aid and
comfort to the wounded hopes and the blighted projects of
the mind.

In the parable story it is a Samaritan who plays the part of
neighbor. The Samaritans were the despised people, half-
breeds, and therefore not considered among the elite of

society. The Jews at Jerusalem were the elite. The mixed
Jews of Samaria and Galilee were looked down upon. Likewise the spiritual law of the inward man is not prominently
accepted among the philosophy and learning of the
world. Man spends millions to study the physical universe,
but very little to study himself. And it is only knowledge of himself which can enable a man to change within
himself, to set the law of liberty in motion, to correct his
bondage, to succor the wounded neighbor among the thieves
in his own mind, and because of this, to raise his own consciousness to that point of gladness and confidence which
will automatically pour itself forth in generosity, tolerance
and magnanimity and mercy to the neighbor on the outside.

THE LAW IS A
PERSON

7

OBEDIENCE AND HUMILITY

―――――

THE PARABLE OF THE CHIEF SEATS

And he put forth a parable to those which were bidden, when he marked how they chose out the chief rooms; saying unto them,

When thou art bidden of any man to a wedding, sit not down in the highest room; lest a more honourable man than thou be bidden of him;

And he that bade thee and him come and say to thee, Give this man place; and thou begin with shame to take the lowest room.

But when thou art bidden, go and sit down in the lowest room; that when he that bade thee cometh, he may say unto thee, Friend, go up higher: then shalt thou have worship in the presence of them that sit at meat with thee.

For whosoever exalteth himself shall be abased; and he that humbleth himself shall be exalted.

Luke 14:7-11

THE ANCIENT RABBIS SAID, "The law is a person," by which they indicated that the law is not just a cold, callous, mathematical thing but has warmth and love as well. Religionists argue over whether God is a person or a principle, when, as a matter of fact, he is both. God is our name for that absolute being in which all opposites are contained, because in an absolute state they have not yet been separated by analysis, division and function. As Judge Troward points out, the very essence of personality is responsiveness, and we have seen in our study of the parables so far how the law is continually responsive to our thought. "Draw nigh unto him and he will draw nigh unto thee," and "I love them that love me." I may address a stone, but I shall get no response from a stone, for it has no personality. But if I speak to a person, I shall get some intelligent response. Hence I have seen how the law responds, intelligently, mathematically and orderly. I know that the law has the element of personality as well as the element of mathematics.

Dr. Frank Crane in a little piece called, "Law," says in part:

> I am law. I am nature's way. I am God's way. . . . The ignorant fear me. They run from my face. They tremble at my voice. But the wise love me and seek me forever. I am their desired lover. Fools think to outwit me and that no Son of man has ever done. I am more clever than the cleverest. I am stronger than the strongest. I am old as God. I never sleep. I never err. I am virile as youth. I am accurate as mathematics. I am beautiful as poetry. I am sweet as music. . . . Heaven is where I am. Hell is where I am not. I am efficiency in man. I am loveliness in woman. . . . I whirl, I dance, I flame, I freeze, but always mathematically, for I am more intricate than calculus, more accurate than any instrument. They that live by me find peace. They that kiss me find love. They that walk with me come at last to God.

The Parable of the Chief Seats

This is an accurate account of man as he is today and as he must always have been while toiling upward toward the light. For without that inner light that shows that the kingdom of heaven is within, a man becomes eager and willful, and even arrogant on the outside. And all of this is to no avail in the end because it is confidence in the wrong procedure, and confidence in the wrong procedure is denial of the right one. So man in his misunderstanding is always hurting himself, and robbing from himself without knowing it.

And so the parable tells plainly how people with the worldly and external point of view act in their effort to attain prominence. There are always people who would rather be thought rich than be rich, who would rather be thought important by the crowd than to be worth anything inside of themselves. The more strenuous a man is in his external efforts to achieve prominence and place among men, the more he tends to deny and to omit the one sure way to acceptance and respect and honor by others, and that is by the development of his own inner integrity. The world is full of those who strive and push for outward position and place at the expense of inner worth. They seem to feel that the old adage of "Assume a virtue if you have it not," means to put on an outward show, to jockey yourself into a position, so that you may appear before men to be what you are not as yet in consciousness.

But the law will not be denied. It thinks with a thousand brains and sees with a thousand eyes. It knows every subtle nuance of your thoughts and moods, and is mathematically aware of your place in consciousness or in the kingdom of heaven. It is quite aware, for example, that a man who feels compelled to elbow his way rudely to the head of the line,

who pushes and scrambles for prominence, who has to promote himself, and who puts his trust and confidence in
badges and credentials of office, that such a man does not
actually believe in himself. The prominence for which he
struggles on the outside is really a confession of a void inside. No matter where or how he exalts himself, the law
will demonstrate itself through his consciousness and through
his consciousness alone, and since his consciousness is one of
lack and inferiority, he will soon have to step down from the
position in which he has placed himself externally. The
harder you try to promote yourself externally, the more you
will succeed in demoting yourself. For promotion comes
from God, and through the law of consciousness. There is no
other kind that is permanent.

For the mental scientist, that craftsman in the kingdom
of heaven whose business is the building of the temple of
God's presence in the individual mind and heart, this parable provides the right methods and the right tools for his
trade. He is interested in attaining the highest room, but not
directly. He knows his primary concern must be with what
goes on in his own mind. His workshop is his own mind.
His tools are his images, and his attitudes and choices. He
knows and works by principle: that all states of consciousness are sooner or later confirmed in fact and function.
Therefore the correct way to find promotion without is to
establish that promotion within in consciousness, and then
to allow the law to confirm itself in outer fact. Such a person
is so sure of this principle that he is utterly humble on the
outside. He has no pride of accomplishment, position, of
person, ancestry or wealth, or of any other quality or characteristic. He knows that all things are done through and by
and in the law. "Of myself I can do nothing; the Father
indwelling he doeth the works."

He knows that if he works with the law and fulfills it inside of himself, the law will set him on high in his external world. He knows that to struggle and strain and to try to force a conclusion by human will and ego alone is to set in motion what has been called the law of reversed effort. Coué used to demonstrate this law scientifically and set it down in this famous saying: "In any battle between the imagination and the will, the imagination will always win." For imagination lays hold of an infinite will which compels all things before it. The person who knows this has no need for human pride, for he possesses the secret of all promotion and accomplishment. He is unafraid to take a low place in society, anywhere. For by scientific prayer and the use of creative imagination he is always going within his own chamber and garmenting himself in the garment of royalty and majesty, announcing his spiritual sovereignty and allowing the eternal law of things to verify and confirm this before men.

Therefore, despise not the day of small things. Learn obedience to the high vision of your greater self within. Be humble, meek and pliable before the great law, and it will raise you up in dignity and in stature. The whole story of Jesus from beginning to end is the biography of this law, embodied in his person, in action. He was born in Galilee, the despised and looked-down-upon province. "Can any good come out of Nazareth?" The very word "Nazareth" means a sprout, something alive but very small and insignificant outwardly. Yet he is God's son and therefore King of kings and Lord of lords, before whom every knee shall bow. Whatever else you may think of Jesus, he represents the greatest truth we can experience.

The parable, therefore, is an illustration of how the true mental scientist must be careful not to exalt himself, else in

doing so he reverses the law and finds himself humbled
But if he humbles himself before the law, he shall be exalted
outwardly.

THE PARABLE OF
THE PHARISEE AND THE PUBLICAN

And he spake this parable unto certain which trusted in
themselves that they were righteous, and despised
others:

Two men went up into the temple to pray; the
one a Pharisee, and the other a publican,

The Pharisee stood and prayed thus with himself,
God, I thank thee, that I am not as other men are, ex-
tortioners, unjust, adulterers, or even as this publican.

I fast twice in the week, I give tithes of all that I
possess.

And the publican, standing afar off, would not lift
so much as his eyes unto heaven, but smote upon his
breast, saying, God be merciful to me a sinner.

I tell you, this man went down to his house justified rather than the other: for every one that exalteth
himself shall be abased; and he that humbleth himself shall be exalted.

Luke 18:9-14

THE PHARISEES once asked Jesus when the kingdom of God
would come, and he answered that "The kingdom of God
cometh not with observation: Neither shall they say, Lo here!
or, lo there! for, behold, the kingdom of God is within you."
(Luke 17:20-21) The kingdom of heaven is an inner state,
not an outer position or place. The kingdom of heaven is a

higher level of consciousness which a man can work up to by realization and awareness. It is a higher level from which a higher authority acts and governs. But as we have seen throughout the parables, the Pharisee is representative of a type of mind which does not understand this. As Maurice Nicol describes him: "The Pharisee represents the man who cannot evolve because he is turned the wrong way around and gets everything upside down. The Pharisee is in externals, in merit, and in the love of external appearances."

All this means, psychologically, that the Pharisee within a man cuts him off from entry into the kingdom. The Pharisee did everything for the sake of appearance. The error of the Pharisee in this parable is that he justifies himself by his outward behavior, and this indicates complete ignorance of the law. The Pharisee, believing that he has arrived, is no longer teachable. He is bound at a certain level of development, for being unwilling to think a new thought, he cannot move into a new and higher level of himself. His sin is in feeling that he is right and others are wrong. His prayers are therefore idle and useless mummeries which get him nowhere. He prays by rote and by vain repetitions. Because he is settled and satisfied, he cannot change or move within himself.

But the publican, like the harlot, is conscious of his own limitation. He is aware of the insufficiency of his own strength and his own merit. He is aware that the human will, unaided, can do little or nothing. He therefore has true humility which makes him receptive to something higher. Because he is receptive, he can receive, and therefore his prayer is effective, because he makes room within himself for the holy guest, the object of his prayer.

When you pray you must be willing to put yourself under orders from on high. You cannot outline and dictate the procedure; you must leave that to the law. But admitting your own human incapacity and relying on the mathematical principle of the law, and the infinite compassion and love of the law as a person, you make room in yourself for the law to work upon you and in you, to take you out of misery and bring you peace and happiness. With this attitude, you will come away from the place of prayer justified. Justified means made right or equitable. When your prayer is answered things are balanced. Desire is satisfied in fulfillment. Yearning and wanting are replaced by, and lost in, satisfaction. When by prayer you establish a new state of consciousness, that new state of consciousness as the authoritative functioning of the law, establishes its physical counterpart, verification and confirmation. And so subjective and objective equal each other. The outside is as the inside. This is justification, and it can come about only through the attitude of humility.

THE PARABLE OF
THE UNPROFITABLE SERVANTS

And the apostles said unto the Lord, Increase our faith.

And the Lord said, If ye had faith as a grain of mustard seed, ye might say unto this sycamine tree, Be thou plucked up by the root, and be thou planted in the sea; and it should obey you.

But which of you, having a servant plowing or feeding cattle, will say unto him by and by, when he is come from the field, Go and sit down to meat?

And will not rather say unto him, Make ready wherewith I may sup, and gird thyself, and serve me, till I have eaten and drunken; and afterward thou shalt eat and drink?

Doth he thank that servant because he did the things that were commanded him? I trow not.

So likewise ye, when ye shall have done all those things which are commanded you, say, We are unprofitable servants: we have done that which was our duty to do.

Luke 17:5-10

"WHO HAS MORE OBEDIENCE than I," says Emerson, "masters me." The whole teaching of Jesus centers around this very point, that mastery is built upon obedience. Elsewhere he has told his disciples not to strive and struggle for position and favor among men or among themselves, but "whosoever would be great among you, let him be your servant." Look around you and you will find this principle enthroned everywhere in the lives of successful men and women. This is a parable about obedience and humility, and teaches one of the most important lessons anyone can possibly know. I think you may agree with me when you finish reading this and the next two parables, and have considered them together, that these may well be considered the most important parables of all in their unadorned simplicity, and they convey the most important piece of information an individual can know for his health and progress and happiness.

All the great people are good servants. Our heroes are people who serve us. We heap honor and praise and fame upon those who work for our benefit. That is the way it is in the society of men. Edison lighted the world, and Marconi enabled us to talk around it. They and all the other great benefactors of the human race are great and honored and famous because they served us. Their lives were productive in behalf of the whole human race. But they were able to serve the race because they served nature first. They guessed and tested, and guessed and tested again, until they found nature's way and brought their thoughts and actions into accord with it. And around the world the maxim of the scientist today is: Nature obeys us in proportion that we first obey nature.

And so obedience is one of the great laws of life. As we said earlier in these pages, each and every one of us is under orders of some kind. The sooner we understand this the happier our lives will be. There is a supreme will over and above our own human wills, and that will is found to master each and every one of us in one way or another, good if we will have it good, ill if we allow it to be so. If we learn the laws of nature and of nature's God, we shall find that they are all for our happiness. It will then be our pleasure to move with them instead of against them. Then they become sovereign masters working for the extension of our good, and it is our joy to be servants of these masters. But if we do not serve them, if we do not devote ourselves to finding out what the laws of life and health and happiness are, and if we therefore do not abide by them, they still remain our masters and they master us in trouble and in defeat because we were not devoted enough to accept something better at their hands.

The Parable of the Unprofitable Servant was told because "the apostles said unto the Lord, Increase our faith." And he immediately made reference to the mustard seed: "If ye had faith as a grain of mustard seed, ye might say unto this sycamine tree, Be thou plucked up by the root, and be thou planted in the sea; and it should obey you." How perfectly marvellous! we might exclaim. Can faith really work such miracles? Faith does everything that is done upon this earth. For faith is the movement of the single and only creative power, in and through the minds of men. Jesus captures the attention and impresses the mind indelibly in this dramatic instance with the power of faith. But he immediately goes on to show that faith is not always an easy acquisition, and it is not like a piece of furniture which, once acquired, lasts for the rest of your life. Faith is something which you work at continuously. You are like a servant, serving your master. You have to keep up the service in order to maintain faith, and only the attitude of devotion or even slavish service to your ideals and the laws of creative thought will maintain the mind in a condition of faith. In prayer and meditation the mind turns away from the reports of the senses, not to ignore them, but in order to balance them with other important information. So the mind turns within and considers the law of all life—as within so without.

We have already seen that the state of the mind may have been depressed by reports from the outside land of the senses. So in considering the law of the creative mind, we relieve the mind of the notion that what the senses report is inevitable. This weakens the sense of fear and doubt somewhat, and makes the mind see that it has a leverage over the events of its life, that it can establish control. The confidence of the mind rises, and the student of things spiritual will go on in his meditation and call to mind all the corollaries of the great creative law. He will remind himself that God said to Moses, and therefore to every human being: "Behold, I have made thee a god to Pharaoh." When he feels enough confidence in the spiritual law of things, he will quietly turn his mind to his particular goal or purpose in life, or his several goals and purposes, or perhaps his supreme over-all strategic objective, and acknowledge its success, and his own joy in that success. He will marry himself to his goal in confidence, and whenever his confidence wanes, he will remind himself that in relation to his particular and individual goals and purposes in life, his mind and only his mind is God, and therefore what he has felt and wanted in its secret chambers in regard to his purposes and goals, is law, incontrovertible and infallible, having its own power to execute itself mathematically, orderly and beautifully, in divine law and order, in harmony with all things and people everywhere.

This kind of a meditation is devotion, and in the terms of the parable, the watchful servant's duty to the master—or the great mind of the universe. It is your duty and it is my duty to engage in something like this every day, to turn to it a thousand times a day, and to tie some portion of every minute and every hour to such meditation. If we do so we cannot fail to build our minds in the image and likeness of that which we image and worship, and to fashion into the fabric of our own consciousness the strength and the peace of the presence of God. The more you feel the presence of God working within your own mind, the more confidence you will feel as you proceed back into the life of the senses, deaf to their predictions of calamity, because you have heard and are hearing another voice with greater authority to announce all things good.

And that is why Jesus compares such service in the mind and in the thought to servants who serve their master night and day, diligently and uncomplainingly, whenever the demand is there. And when they have done that, they have done only their duty. To be a good servant is no small and easy task. It requires skill of mind and heart as well as of hand. It is the duty of a good servant to serve his master or employer, day or night, and uncomplainingly. His duties may be heavy, but so long as they are not unjust they are his duties, and a good servant will perform them in such a way that they become a privilege, as well as a duty. Any man, whether he works for another or for himself, if he does the job industriously and uncomplainingly, becomes a free man in that job. And that feeling of freedom will lead him to higher things. But the worker who thinks that labor is a curse, and who spends too much time in comparing himself and his goods with other men and their goods, is a slave in his job, and the slavery, which is in his mind alone, will lead him into wider degrees of servitude.

Your purpose, goal and vision in life should be your real master, is, in fact, your master. Serve him loyally and devotedly, and you will have the blessings of life. All of this is confirmed and reemphasized in the following parables.

THE PARABLE OF
THE TRAVELLING HOUSEHOLDER

Take ye heed, watch and pray: for ye know not when the time is.

For the Son of man is as a man taking a far journey, who left his house, and gave authority to his servants, and to every man his work, and commanded the porter to watch.

Watch ye therefore: for ye know not when the master of the house cometh, at even, or at midnight, or at the cockcrowing, or in the morning:

Lest coming suddenly he find you sleeping.

And what I say unto you I say unto all, Watch.

Mark 13:33-37

"LET NEITHER DAY nor night unhallowed pass, but still remember what the Lord has done," says Shakespeare, and that, too, is the message of this parable.

Its theme is: Watch. The whole accent of this parable is on watchful alertness. Alertness to what? To the coming good, rather than any impending evil. It is a law of the mind that the mind tends to reproduce what it looks upon, and that is why vision leads all of the faculties. What you look upon, either inwardly or outwardly, you will think about, and what you have thoughts about, you will have feelings about, for one will call forth the other, until you have a whole chain of consciousness about the fact which you first approached through vision alone.

This is a demonstrable law of the mind, and every spiritual scientist must be constantly aware of it. Thinking along the same line builds up a reaction. That reaction, when it comes, is in conformance with the law of heaven. It is a subconscious power, and compulsory; a second nature or an automatic movement. All skill is the acquisition of control over our unconscious forces. When you first learn to play a musical instrument your mind knows what you want to do in an ideal way, but your fingers are awkward and inept. They do not go where your mind knows they should go. But you practice, and you devote yourself to the ideal, and then one day a miracle takes place. Facility and ease creep into and through your fingers. They move of themselves. There is no longer such thought-taking. It is as though another element has come into your work and is taking it over. This is the principle of all learning, and the principle of the development of all skills. We devote our minds to a certain purpose. We are loyal and patient in devotion, and then the purpose accomplishes itself. We call it second nature. And indeed, it is a second nature, dormant within us all, and wakening into activity only because we desire it and welcome it. "Behold, I stand at the door, and knock: if any man hear my voice, and open the door, I will come in to him, and will sup with him, and he with me."

Immense energies lie dormant in every individual. A greater self is there behind the little self, and the teaching of Jesus is a commentary on the means and methods necessary to bring that greater self into focus and conscious activity.

In much of his teaching he identifies himself with that greater self of all men, and says: "Come unto me all ye that labor and are heavy laden, and I will give you rest." Considering it from another point of view, you may say that there is a great self deep within you which bids you come to it in attention and devotion. Come to it as a servant and feed it your expectancy, your praise, your love and all the emphasis of your mind. There will come a time when it will come forth and do your job for you. At least we may say that it will ease your burden tremendously, and carry much of your load. It will, indeed, give you rest. Speaking psychologically, it is the reaction and the emergence of something which is subconscious or unconscious within you. Speaking Biblically, it is the coming of the Lord, or the coming of the Lord's Day. For it is the coming of a ruling state of consciousness. Every reaction from the subconscious is compulsory, as we have said, and therefore it is sovereign in all the affairs of the individual. It is therefore called the Lord in the Bible. The reaction of the ideal and spiritual life, the emergence of it into the affairs of the personality, is called the Lord, or the coming of the Lord. For there be lords many and gods many, as Paul observes, but we know only one Lord. And that is the lord of good, the lord of beauty, the lord of peace and health and happiness.

"But of that day and that hour knoweth no man, no, not the angels which are in heaven, neither the Son, but the Father." And this state of spiritual and mental affairs is compared in the parable with the fact that the servants in the household who are keeping it ready for the return of their master, do not know precisely when their master will return. They must be alert and watch for the slightest indication of his coming, or else they will be punished when he does come. The lord is always returning, for always there is some reaction from the unconscious or spiritual side of life in terms of the content of the mind. If the mind through sleepiness and laziness becomes negative, it is a vacuum, and the reaction is in kind. That means the reaction to a negative mind is in terms of loss and limitation. Therefore, the parable warns the mind to be alert for one thing, its true ruler, a high vision and a high hope based upon spiritual principles. The happy results of such visioning and such thinking are demonstrated in arresting and dramatic imagery in the next parable.

THE PARABLE OF
THE LORD'S RETURN FROM THE WEDDING

Let your loins be girded about, and your lights burning;
 And ye yourselves like unto men that wait for their lord, when he will return from the wedding; that when he cometh and knocketh, they may open unto him immediately.
 Blessed are those servants, whom the lord when he cometh shall find watching: verily I say unto you, that he shall gird himself, and make them to sit down to meat, and will come forth and serve them.
 And if he shall come in the second watch, or come in the third watch, and find them so, blessed are those servants.
 And this know, that if the goodman of the house had known what hour the thief would come, he would have watched, and not have suffered his house to be broken through.
 Be ye therefore ready also: for the Son of man cometh at an hour when ye think not.

Then Peter said unto him, Lord, speakest thou this parable unto us, or even to all?

And the Lord said, Who then is that faithful and wise steward, whom his lord shall make ruler over his household, to give them their portion of meat in due season?

Blessed is that servant, whom his lord when he cometh shall find so doing.

Of a truth I say unto you, that he will make him ruler over all that he hath.

Luke 12:35-44

THIS PARABLE has much the same base as the ones we have just discussed with one important difference. It is peculiar to Luke and it stresses some of the most dramatic imagery which Jesus used, the reaction of the law to a watchful and constructive mind. If the servants or faculties of the mind hold and work with a constructive vision, then the reaction of the law will be constructive and pleasing. Servants who do their job well will find their positions exactly reversed when the Lord returns. The Lord will be their servant, and will cause them all to sit down in the kingdom of heaven and the Lord will minister unto them.

Now this is exactly what Jesus did at the Last Supper when he laid aside his garments and girded himself with a towel and washed the feet of the disciples. Here is a strong portrayal of the great and fundamental law of all nature as well as of our own minds. The powerful forces of nature such as steam, electricity and atomic energy are all our servants today because we have first been their servants. Men and women have devoted long hours of research into natural phenomena to determine the laws of nature, and then to plan and to build in accordance with those laws. The response we get from the great forces of nature is like a bless-

ing. The law is always reciprocal. As we understand the
forces of nature, so they will act for us, and the same is true
of the highest laws of God's kingdom.

Our experiences are the reactions of our thoughts. If we
study to make our thoughts constructive and persist in devoting the mind to a high vision, if we build up confidence in the
higher workings of the mind, then one result and only one result is inevitable, and that is that every obstacle, and every
natural difficulty will move aside from the path of the man
who has faith. For the man who has faith will have power,
and the power is the reaction of his faith. It is the returning
of the Lord. It is the ruling authority of the thing that you
have worshiped and idealized.

One of the most practical ways in which a person can
make use of this understanding of the law is in the breaking
of old habits and the establishment of new. I have taught
many people, for example, to stop smoking by the application
of this principle. Whilst one is in the grip of a bad habit
one's will power is weak and ineffective, but by desiring to
be free, by visioning oneself as free, by constantly reminding
oneself that such thinking and visioning builds up reactions from the unconscious side of life which, when they
arise, compel toward good with the same force that they
formerly compelled toward error—by this means one can
build a new habit structure into the mind, and by the reaction of the law of the mind this new structure will precipitate itself into function and into experience. Anybody can
have will power, not by struggling against his habit or any
fact or any situation in his life, but by going within, devoting
himself to a vision of what he wants to be, and building it
up thought by thought and mood by mood, until the vessel
of consciousness is so full of a certain kind and quality of
thought that it passes from vision and ideal into function
and fact. Anybody can have anything by this means.

The Lord, or the reaction of the law, is always coming, and when he comes he deals with you exactly as you dealt with him. So "Let your loins be girded about," that is, put on the confidence of your strength in the law; and "your lights burning," that is, your perception and understanding of the law of things clear and penetrating; and be "yourselves like unto men that wait for their lord, when he will return from the wedding." In other words, be a good servant and you shall be served.

REALIZATION
AND
ATTAINMENT

8

THE LAW OF LIFE

THE PARABLE OF
THE LOST SHEEP AND THE LOST COIN

And he spake this parable unto them, saying,

    What man of you, having an hundred sheep, if he lose one of them, doth not leave the ninety and nine in the wilderness, and go after that which is lost, until he find it?

    And when he hath found it, he layeth it on his shoulders, rejoicing.

    And when he cometh home, he calleth together his friends and neighbours, saying unto them, Rejoice with me; for I have found my sheep which was lost.

    I say unto you, that likewise joy shall be in heaven over one sinner that repenteth, more than over ninety and nine just persons, which need no repentance.

    Either what woman having ten pieces of silver, if

she lose one piece, doth not light a candle, and sweep
the house, and seek diligently till she find it?

And when she hath found it, she calleth her friends
and her neighbours together, saying, Rejoice with
me; for I have found the piece which I had lost.

Likewise, I say unto you, there is joy in the presence of the angels of God over one sinner that re-
penteth.

Luke 15:3-10

WE ARE DRAWING to the close of our study of the parables,
or our study of the divine law in ourselves. We should have
gained a treasure in our reading, and that treasure, of course,
is the law of life itself. It is the one thing worth while because all other things depend upon it. Being born into the
land of experience and matter deprives us somewhat of the
awareness of this law, and so the consciousness of it is said
to have been lost. And the story of the Bible, as the spiritual
history of man, or the history of spiritual man, is the story of
seeking and finding that which was lost. "The son of man
came to seek and to save that which was lost," and with the
finding of that one thing there is realization and attainment
and rejoicing. The last two parables tell us about this.

The only begotten Son of God is the mind and consciousness of God, and Paul says: "Let this mind which was in
Christ Jesus be also in you." What, then, is the significance
of this parable which a man who has a hundred sheep, would
leave ninety-nine of them and go and seek one that was
lost? And why does the second half of the parable mention
a woman having ten pieces of silver and losing one, and
turning the house upside down until she finds it? Because
these illustrations of finding lost items in the world are figures of the one significant enterprise of our lives, namely, the
search for and the finding of the One, the creative presence

within ourselves. This is our real task, and when we sense
it we leave all else to accomplish it. This is our over-all purpose and task in life, to search for and to find the One, and
his law. But it is also our daily task.

Every life faces its daily problems, situations to be
adjusted, obstacles to be overcome. If one is thinking spiritually and therefore constructively, he is constantly on the
lookout for the good part in every situation, and he is su-
premely concerned with holding on to that good part in his
mind as a consciousness of success and health and happiness.
The details of one's daily life are not nearly so important as
this consciousness. Keep this, and you keep all; lose this,
and you lose all.

All through the Bible the sheep and the shepherd are
symbols of the spiritual mind. The chief belief or dominant
conviction in the mind is the shepherd which shepherds all
the thoughts and moods and attitudes and outlooks of the
mind. Ideally, the consciousness of the law and the presence
of God should be the dominant shepherd of the consciousness. That is why Jesus speaks of himself as the good shepherd, for the spiritual mind alone can shepherd and
keep the parts of consciousness in health and harmony.
A false belief is a false shepherd which allows the sheep
to be devoured by the wolves of fear, avarice and anxiety. The spiritual shepherd is always on guard that he
lose none of his sheep to the ugly emotions of the outside
world. When his hope or his confidence wanders away, he
is quick about it to bring it back to the fold. He will leave
ninety-and-nine stable emotions to work upon one that is
unstable until he gets it associated harmoniously with the
whole plan and purpose of his life.

To jump to the analogy in the second part of the parable,
if the spiritual thinker loses any part of his purchase upon
life's problems, symbolized in the parable by the woman

losing the money, he will work over his own mind and turn
it upside down until he finds that part once more and rests
secure, so that with the rest of his treasures of confidence
and faith he can demand and buy the good things of life.

An old Persian parable will help, perhaps, to point up further the meaning to the parable of things that were lost: A
man died and went to heaven's gate. He was told by the guardian angel there that he could enter only when he had brought
earth's most prized possession. So the man went away and
returned bringing the matchless jewels of King Cyrus'
crown. And the guard said: "The streets of this city are
paved with gold and its walls are of precious stones." The
man went away a second time and returned, bringing with
him the sword of Alexander, conqueror of the world. And
the answer from the guard this time was: "Alexander is
dust. The least of our messengers slew him in his frailty.
Earth's strength is weakness here." The man left heaven's
gate for the third time, and returned to earth to seek for
earth's most prized possession. This time he brought with
him the lost books of Solomon's wisdom, and the guardian
angel replied: "Man's wisdom is folly in heaven where all
things are known fully." At last the man came to heaven's
gate and brought nothing, and the angel let him in.

In all of our earth life there is only one thing to seek for
and only one thing to find, and that is the consciousness of
God's presence. The knowledge of the law gives us this.
But consciousness is no thing, and therefore it is no thing,
or nothing, which opens for us the gates of heaven. In spite
of the thousands of years of Biblical instruction and other
similar instruction, millions still spend their lives trying to
gather and to accumulate and to hold fast the dust of the
earth in the form of money and jewels and houses and lands,
influence and power. In spite of the fact that, as one of our
preceding parables pointed out, people have Moses and the

prophets and they have Jesus, and they have the accumulated spiritual teaching of many minds and saviours, they still do not have the son of God himself, or the consciousness of God's presence. The millions who strive and war for the treasures of the earth still do not know the law. All that a man accumulates of earthly property will at the moment he draws his last breath belong to somebody else. We can take nothing over except what we are. We pass from room to room in the Father's house of universal consciousness by means of what we know inside of ourselves. Therefore with all thy getting get understanding. Understanding buys any other gift or quality of life.

THE PARABLE OF THE PRODIGAL SON

And he said, a certain man had two sons:

And the younger of them said to his father, Father, give me the portion of goods that falleth to me. And he divided unto them his living.

And not many days after the younger son gathered all together, and took his journey into a far country, and there wasted his substance with riotous living.

And when he had spent all, there arose a mighty famine in that land; and he began to be in want.

And he went and joined himself to a citizen of that country; and he sent him into his fields to feed swine.

And he would fain have filled his belly with the husks that the swine did eat: and no man gave unto him.

And when he came to himself, he said, How many hired servants of my father's have bread enough and to spare, and I perish with hunger!

I will arise and go to my father, and will say unto him, Father, I have sinned against heaven, and before thee,

And am no more worthy to be called thy son: make me as one of thy hired servants.

And he arose, and came to his father. But when he was yet a great way off, his father saw him, and had compassion, and ran, and fell on his neck, and kissed him.

And the son said unto him, Father, I have sinned against heaven, and in thy sight, and am no more worthy to be called thy son.

But the father said to his servants, Bring forth the best robe, and put it on him; and put a ring on his hand, and shoes on his feet:

And bring hither the fatted calf, and kill it; and let us eat, and be merry:

For this my son was dead, and is alive again; he was lost, and is found. And they began to be merry.

Now his elder son was in the field: and as he came and drew nigh to the house, he heard musick and dancing.

And he called one of the servants, and asked what these things meant.

And he said unto him, Thy brother is come; and thy father hath killed the fatted calf, because he hath received him safe and sound.

And he was angry, and would not go in: therefore came his father out, and intreated him.

And he answering said to his father, Lo, these many years do I serve thee, neither transgressed I at any time thy commandment: and yet thou never gavest me a kid, that I might make merry with my friends:

But as soon as this thy son was come, which hath
devoured thy living with harlots, thou hast killed for
him the fatted calf.

And he said unto him, Son, thou art ever with me,
and all that I have is thine.

It was meet that we should make merry, and be
glad: for this thy brother was dead, and is alive
again; and was lost, and is found.

Luke 15:11-32

THE LAST PARABLE for our consideration is a jewel of the
Bible and of literature. It is outstanding from any point of
view. Its humanness and tenderness, and its obvious truth-
fulness have touched men deeply for hundreds of years.

This is a parable; therefore it states two parallel truths.
One set of facts is obvious, being the story itself, an account
of family life which is repeated over and over again around
the world every day of our lives. The other set of facts is
implied by the narrative. Let us proceed to the implied
inner meaning. A certain man had two sons is a way of
saying that life has two parts, or two directions. This is a
universal law. Some names for the two parts are: matter and
spirit, material and immaterial, visible and invisible, inside
and outside, positive and negative, up and down, and so
forth.

Narrowing the meaning still more, the phrase: "a certain
man had two sons," is a way of describing you and me. Each
of us has two sides to his nature, two directions in which we
can use the force of our mind. There is a natural side and
an ideal side to each and every one of us. The natural side
is born first. That is the elder brother: the ordinary mind,
with its ordinary awareness of ordinary conditions and surroundings and situations. The elder brother is satisfied to
remain at home. That part of the mind which is dissatisfied,

which is idealistic, which is young and full of desire and zeal, but nevertheless without discretion, without skill or knowledge—this is the younger brother. This is the youthful and exuberant part of the mind. It is not content to live with old forms and situations. It senses that the way of change is the way of progress. The elder brother is conservative. The younger is radical. Yet this younger brother part of us is the only means by which we make progress. It is rash and foolish and gets into trouble. It wastes our substance. But in the end it saves us.

Whenever life hands you some problem which requires some change of thought and action on your part, the younger son is leaving home. For the ideal part of the mind no longer rests with the facts of your life, but with some ideal or more desirable state. The younger son says to his father, "Give me the portion of goods that falleth to me." Whenever the human mind desires something better than it is now experiencing, the younger son is leaving home and the father is dividing his goods with him. That is, the mind or the consciousness which stands behind and gives rise to the two directional tendencies of the mind, is putting a certain amount of its interest and its feeling, its hope and its confidence, in the younger son. A certain portion of the force of the mind goes with the ideal; not all of it, not even half of it. In our society the elder son usually gets the greater proportion of his father's goods, and psychologically this is true also. Most of the force of the mind stays to maintain the status quo. A lesser portion of the mind goes with the ideal in hope of better things.

From here on the story of the younger son is the story of nearly every human life in its search for spiritual maturity. Before we know the spiritual law and how to live with it and work with it, we make many false starts and waste our energies in many false practices. We discover right off that the physical facts of life contradict our idealism, and immediately we have a quarrel on our hands. We yearn, we wish, we desire, we hope, but always some cruel set of facts destroys our hope and frustrates our aim. The material facts seem to preclude the realization of our ideal. As this conflict deepens the mind becomes involved with many illusions and false beliefs, such as the belief in material causation, and as this happens the mind is drawn further and further away from the source of creation which is consciousness and consciousness alone. The ideal, as it first speaks to us inside of our minds, is really the voice of God. It is the Word which is with God in the beginning, and that Word becomes flesh in a mind that has spiritual confidence. But the mind that does not know this as yet goes out to seek the ideal, and becomes impressed with the formidable array of facts and situations opposing it. These inspire the mind's thinking and condition its feelings until finally hopelessness and despair, fear and anxiety, bear down and deplete the zeal and the power of the ideal. The mind is spending its money now and losing its force. It is getting deeper and deeper into confusion. And this is what is figured in the parable by the story of the younger son going into a far country, away from the spiritual home, out into the wilderness of matter, and there wasting his substance with riotous living.

The picture of the young man dissipating and carousing which is so often drawn from this part of the parable, and upon which too many commentators dwell too long, is only the outside structure of the story and contains no particular enlightenment for us. It is a story which is happening perennially. At this hour thousands of young men are literally and physically spending their inheritance of money, drinking and carousing, and sowing their wild oats. In a year or two they will tire of it all, learn the emptiness of it all, and settle down to productive living. If this were all there were to the

parable, it would not be more significant than a hundred
other stories in our literature. But because it is a parable,
careful reading should arouse the parallel meaning in our
minds. When youthful exuberance and zeal are spent, and
when conditions and circumstances have worn down one's
desire and hope until it is like only a flickering candle flame,
then comes the time in the consciousness described in the
parable as: "there arose a mighty famine in that land, and
he began to be in want."

To be in health the mind must feed upon images and prospects of good. So long as it has a strong and healthy and
vibrant ideal, and a few reasons for holding to it, it will feed
upon these. And so long as outer conditions do not contradict the ideal too much, there is some cheer in the environment itself. But when the ideal wears thin, and when the
outer conditions are threatening, then the mind has no where
to turn for food, and there is indeed a famine in that land.
Then the parable says that the young man "came to himself," and in this sentence alone you have the revelation that
he had been traveling away from himself. So the young man
came to himself and he began to think of home.

This is a figure of the human mind which has been thrown
back upon itself and discovers its own resources, and a
wisdom and a power native to the self which it had overlooked before. The wisdom and power necessary for every
human life comes along with that life at birth and never
leaves it. It is hidden in the chambers of the soul and every
mind must learn how to travel back to that home of his life
and find his source and sustenance again.

Every emergency like this proves the truth that the Bible
teaches, that God is in man, and God is available to man,
and God is the highest and the best of everything that man
is. "I, the imperfect," says Emerson, "adore my own perfect." And in the figure of the parable the young man stops

in his tracks and begins to adore his own perfect. Suffering
and misery have this virtue, that they tend to open up the
mind to self-discovery and self-realization. And so after his
great suffering the young man sees by contrast the meaning
of the life he has left. There is born in the mind at this
juncture the awareness of the spiritual cause as transcendent
of all other so-called causes, the discovery that thoughts are
things, that, as Plato said, "Our mind is God." These and
many other new awarenesses come streaming into the mind
to fill it with an awareness of the divine law and a consciousness of the divine presence.

In the spiritual sense of the parable, this awareness is automatically the Father's house, for the mind is home again
in its own integrity, wrapped in its own self-chosen garments
of praise and holiness and cleanliness, free from the badger-
ing taunts and torments of materiality, living above the fogs
and the damps of purely externalistic experience. The moment this realization comes to the mind there is a great reaction from the other side of life. The Father comes to meet
his son. And as there is rejoicing in the personal and individual mind which has discovered the light and the truth
of its own being, so there is equal rejoicing in the universal
or Father side of life, for just as a father finds great joy in
the successes of his son, so the universal life can be said to
find its greatest pleasure in the success of its projections and
creations.

What is figured in the return of the lord from the wedding
when he sits down to serve his servant is also figured in the
story of the father coming out to meet his son, killing the
fatted calf, ordering a robe and a ring to be fetched for
the son.

There is one point left in the parable, and that is the
graceless performance of the elder brother at the celebration
of the younger brother's return. He was angry and jealous

and remonstrated with his father for heaping these honors upon his younger brother. He felt that it was all unjust. That he did not love his brother is evident in the fact that he refers to him in the presence of the father as "thy son." He points out that: "Lo, these many years do I serve thee, neither transgressed I at any time thy commandment: and yet thou never gavest me a kid, that I might make merry with my friends." He points out all of his own virtues and emphasizes that he never transgressed. This reminds us of that truth that we have already discussed, namely, that a negative kind of goodness is not goodness at all. Failure to do wrong is not necessarily doing right.

The elder brother, in the science of the mind, represents, as we have indicated, that conservative, standpat attitude in contrast to the idealism represented by the younger brother. He has accepted the status quo, so he can't get into trouble because he has no disagreements. He sees nothing better or beyond what he has now, therefore he has no disire or ideal, and he is happy with what is. But because he has no ideal, he can never grow; because he cannot grow, he cannot learn to know the spiritual law. The return of the prodigal, like the repentance of one sinner, causes more rejoicing in the kingdom of heaven for the reason that return to the father's house, and repentance, which are the same thing, mean self-discovery, illumination and self-realization. They represent, therefore, an order and a level of life far above and beyond that level and order represented by the elder brother. Here again is the evidence of that truth that Jesus has repeatedly stated: the first shall be last and the last shall be first.

How many never fly simply because they do not try their wings! How many enterprises are lost because of hesitancy to attempt! This principle of self-reliance and inner native capacity is illustrated by a little story that is going about: A frog

fell into a deep rut on a muddy road. He jumped and jumped
in an effort to get out, but to no avail. His friends stood
around and watched and sympathized, but when evening
fell they all went home, leaving the frog in the deep rut.
When morning came they all returned and found the frog
sitting on the side of the road chirping a song of victory in
the sunlight. His friends all inquired, "How did you get out
of that hole?" He replied, "A truck came along and I had to
get out."

The elder brother is the old intellect, unillumined, unredeemed and unchanged. It still thinks the same old thoughts
and moves in the same old track. It won't believe in the new
revelation, and therefore it cannot rejoice that the lost is
found. It never can see the superiority of the spiritual element, and so it sees no cause for rejoicing that this has been
recovered. It ignorantly assumes that it could have received
the father's gifts if they had been offered. But it could not
receive special honors, for it had done nothing to deserve
special honors. But it is in the father's house and is necessary
to life and will continue so long as human beings continue.
As was said about Cain, the first incarnation of evil among
men, the Lord set a mark upon Cain that no one should kill
him, and he lives still today. Again, the divine wisdom
made a distinction between the two sons of Abraham, Isaac
and Ishmael, the one by a bondmaid, the other by a freewoman. As Paul says: ". . . he who was of the bondwoman
was born after the flesh; but he of the freewoman was by
promise." (Galatians 4:23) "Which things are an allegory:
for these are the two covenants; . . . Cast out the bondwoman
and her son: for the son of the bondwoman shall not be heir
with the son of the freewoman." (Galatians 4:24, 30) But
in spite of the fact that Ishmael was cast out, he was not
destroyed for the divine wisdom speaks to his mother and

says: "Arise, lift up the lad, and hold him in thine hand; for I will make him a great nation." (Genesis 21:18)

Throughout the Bible the distinction between the two types of mind is made repeatedly, and the story of the prodigal son is one of the last instances in the Bible. The elder son lives in the midst of riches but does not really know it. He is not aware of his own blessings, therefore cannot count them. His father says: "Son, thou art ever with me, all that I have is thine," but his attitudes and actions upon the return of his brother prove that he does not understand this. The mind that does not recognize its own worth cannot possibly make use of its riches. The younger brother is an example of that part of the mind which ventures forth, gets hurt, but in the process learns, and its learning enables it to appropriate the father's good. And so to this mind is given the fatted calf, the robe and the ring, the emblems of honor and sovereignty.

So in a few words the parable says, you must believe in you. Your zeal and hope must come back from the thralldom of matter, and recognize the spirit as their saviour. Your intellect must find it reasonable to rejoice in this, and with the happy father sing that song of realization and attainment, confirmation and victory: "This thy brother was dead, and is alive again; and was lost, and is found." For when the younger brother, the ability to think constructively, is alive again, then the business of life can go on; not until then. With the younger brother at home again in the father's house, or in the working consciousness of the mind, there is no problem, no difficulty, no sorrow, no grief that cannot be overcome.

The parables are stories illustrating our own personal enfranchisement, the coming into our lives of the Lord Jesus Christ.